DR. SEBI
SPEAKS OF DEMBALI

DR. SEBI
SPEAKS OF DEMBALI

Crossing Over from Dis-Ease to Ease
in Matters of Health, Race, Family,
and Culture

BEVERLY OLIVER

Dr. Sebi Speaks of Dembali. Copyright © 2019 by Beverly Oliver. All Rights Reserved. No part of this publication may be reproduced, distributed, or transmitted in any form or by any means, including photocopying, recording, digital scanning, or other electronic or mechanical methods, without the prior written permission of the publisher, except in the case of brief quotations embodied in critical reviews and certain other noncommercial uses permitted by copyright law. For more information contact JBDavid Communications, 10063 Riverside Drive #2025, Toluca Lake, CA 91610.

Design by Andrea Reider
Cover by BookBaby
Photographs courtesy of Beverly Oliver
Diagnostic Sheets and The Fig Tree ads courtesy of Dr. Sebi

Published 2020
Printed in the United States of America
Library of Congress Control Number:
       2020909627
ISBN: 978-0-578-69948-6

From the depths of my soul I vowed to leave
asthma at youth's doorstep. It would not cross
the threshold of adulthood. Time's up. So naturally,
my asthma-riddled body conjured him up.
I'm all the better for it.

Contents

ACKNOWLEDGMENTS ix
FOREWORD xi
INTRODUCTION xvii

CHAPTER ONE
FROM THE RAINFOREST TO THE USA 1
Section 1—Biography 1

Alfredo, the River, and the Rain 1
On Our Way to La Ceiba 10
Alfredo's Birth Bed 18
A Street Corner in La Ceiba 24
Black Women Encourage His Healing Journey 29
Los Angeles and the Letter to Elijah Muhammad 36

Section 2—His Work 43
Natural Healing on Trial 43
Healing's Duality: Rejection and Acceptance 51

CHAPTER TWO
ON MATTERS OF RACE 63
Code of Ethics and Race 66
Race and Resonance Matter—Resonance More 68

CONTENTS

CHAPTER THREE
ON MATTERS OF CULTURE 83
Dr. Frances Cress Welsing............................... 85
Anthropology and Human Progression.................. 92
Hippocrates Validated African Herbs 98
A Culture of Bare Feet and Independence 104

CHAPTER FOUR
ON MATTERS OF IDENTITY.......................... 109
The Nuances of Black Identity.......................... 113
Humble, Frank, with a Tinge of Vulgarity 115

CHAPTER FIVE
ON MATTERS OF FOOD AND HEALTH 123
Cassava's Hidden Nature 126
Alkaline Food—A Nourisher........................... 126

CHAPTER SIX
COSMIC ARRANGEMENT OF LIFE 129

CHAPTER SEVEN
USHA VILLAGE 2008—DR. SEBI, HIS GUESTS,
AND DEMBALI.. 133
In the Land of Krishna and Buddha.................... 152
Origins of Disease...................................... 156
Back to Ease 162

EPILOGUE... 171
NOTES.. 173
BIBLIOGRAPHY.. 179

Acknowledgments

To the team that helped build this work, thank you. I am eternally grateful. From the beginning Pamela Ferrell nudged me forward. She constantly probed my "reasons why" so that the answers manifested a book that transported you into Dr. Sebi and Beverly's world—a place where you peer into, query, and understand Dr. Sebi's view of life and all of its complexities. Naomi Eagleson, editorial director of The Artful Editor, provided excellent, hawk-eyed editors, namely expert line editor Denise Logsdon; many thanks also to Ernesto Mestre, Christine Van Zandt, and Christina Palaia, whose initial review helped create the framework for *Dembali's* growth. Matun née Patsy Chapman sat front and center as Dr. Sebi spoke of dembali and approved her inclusion in this book. To Sebi, my friend, brother, teacher, thank you for understanding the black psyche and for your quest to make it whole and healthy again.

Foreword

If you could spend a day with Alfredo Darrington Bowman, a.k.a. Dr. Sebi, or be a butterfly on his wall, you would learn something about yourself and human nature. *Dr. Sebi Speaks of Dembali* is Dr. Sebi's words on matters that go beyond healing. Author Beverly Oliver writes about her experience hanging out with Dr. Sebi to capture a biographical glimpse of his day-to-day life growing up in Honduras, his world travels, and his reflections on human nature. When you look for a message of healing from Dr. Sebi in this book, you'll find he is more passionate about a discussion of *dembali*. Dembali is a word Dr. Sebi often used to define people who reject that which is good for them. He wrestled with the fact that he cured AIDS, cancer, diabetes, and even sickle cell anemia. Rather than any fanfare, he was rejected by African leaders, African American politicians, a skeptical medical industry, and the church.

If we study the lives of prophets Jesus, Moses, and Muhammad, they too were rejected and persecuted for bringing a message of good to people. It seems to be the condition of humanity to distrust the very thing that will make life better for us.

I know firsthand it is not easy being a pioneer. It is not easy to get people to embrace and love their natural self, let alone natural healing. In the 1980s the D.C. Department of

Consumer and Regulatory Affairs attempted to shut down my natural hair care salon, Cornrows & Co., four times and outlawed African hair in its natural state, the way it grows from our scalps. Likewise, the Supreme Court of the State of New York attempted to stop Dr. Sebi from not only healing but from free speech, for saying he cured diseases. He developed the African Bio Mineral Balance system, a system that complements the African genome using plants that God made, the same plants revealed in the Bible and the Qu'ran. Unfortunately, some of us distrust what God provides and have more faith in the chemicals that man makes.

The first time I met Dr. Sebi was in the early 1980s, at his Washington, D.C. office. My husband, Taalib-din, my cousin Tonette, and I went to see him after driving eight hours from Rhode Island. We were returning to D.C. after a family vacation. During the long car ride, Tonette, a Howard University freshman at the time, lay in a fetal position on the back seat crying with intense pain. Eight long hours of it. I didn't know what to do. Going to the hospital was not even a thought, and health insurance didn't exist for us. I don't even remember how I knew about Dr. Sebi. It must have been word of mouth. When we arrived at his office, we were ushered into a room where he sat behind a desk. After we explained how Tonette was feeling, he left the room and came back in ten minutes with a cup of brown liquid. He told Tonette to drink it. She gagged and spit up, not even questioning what was happening because she was so desperate for relief. We left Dr. Sebi's office after thirty minutes. Tonette was pain-free, and a week later, to her surprise, her menstrual cycle came with no cramps.

Twenty-five years would pass before I saw Dr. Sebi again. Thinking back, it was more than healing. It was a friendship. He and I talked for hours on the phone from Washington,

D.C. to Honduras, using phone cards that would expire in mid-sentence.

It was not easy having a persona larger than life, but that was indeed Dr. Sebi—a sharp intellect with a passion for healing and quick to deliver the message of Africa's contribution to natural medicine. He knew that other nationalities were recognized for their natural approach to medicine, but he felt Africa's contributions were ignored. He said even men like Hippocrates learned from Africans.

In 2011 I walked through the rainforest in La Ceiba with Dr. Sebi as he identified plants he used for healing. Honduras is where he expressed to me his ideas of how women would bring healing to the world. I enjoyed our friendship and feel his presence urging me to not let his work be minimized.

His conversations with Beverly leave us with the idea that we have within us the power and freedom to stand in our truth, to embrace the "cosmic order of life," and to stand up to systems that influence how we think, behave, and eat. Dr. Sebi was intense and unapologetic as he made his mark on history. In *Dr. Sebi Speaks of Dembali* his message is not lost, and his words are not distorted.

—Pamela Ferrell

Alfredo Bowman (Dr. Sebi)
on the island of Roatán, Honduras, 2008

Introduction

An occupational hazard of a writer or producer is falling in love with sections of one's work that might end up in a digital trash can or on the studio floor. In media and the entertainment industry, we call this hold-for-possible-use-later material "outtakes." And so it is with material about herbal medicine specialist Dr. Sebi [SAY-BEE], that autodidactic, extraordinary individual legally named Alfredo Darrington Bowman (1933–2016). I'm honored that I knew him personally and well enough to call him Sebi.

He'd have told you his life is an open book. That's the problem. Any attempt to capture Dr. Sebi in totality, no matter how diligent, merely scratches the surface of his true character. His was a life that requires many books: a textbook, a cookbook, a collection of short stories, and a book he decided to write—an autobiography.

In 2005 I traveled to Usha, Dr. Sebi's healing center in La Ceiba, Honduras, to help him fine-tune his unpublished memoir, *The Cure: The Autobiography of Dr. Sebi "Mama Hay"*, a page-turning story from beginning to end. While assisting him, I conducted and recorded a series of interviews over a week. His memoir, just as distinctive and multileveled as its subject, addresses several topics: plants, herbs, and sickle cell anemia; the composition and pH rating of food; his voyages around the world; his second wife, Maa, who co-founded his company, The Fig Tree; the first time he removed the HIV/AIDS virus from a client; his jail time in Brooklyn; and a woman whose influence marked him for life—his grandmother, Mama Hay. Stories within a story is the best description for his memoir. The content of the book greatly influenced our conversations.

That seven-day interview, though biographical in content, contained urgent sociocultural and socioeconomic information useful to the public, particularly black people, according to Dr. Sebi. Many times in our conversations, whether we were sitting in his cabin at Usha or riding around La Ceiba in his mini truck, he'd emphasize the importance of what he had to say. "I want you to write it and put it in the book exactly as I say it" or "And I want to read that in this book." Well, the time has come to honor Dr. Sebi's wishes and include his unpublished insights in today's dialogue about race, identity, health, and culture.

Sometime between the publication of my first two books, *Seven Days in Usha Village: A Conversation with Dr. Sebi* (2007) and *Sojourn to Honduras Sojourn to Healing* (2010)—the first published to commemorate the twentieth anniversary of Dr. Sebi's acquittal for charges of practicing medicine without a license in New York; the second broadening the details of my 2005 visit to Honduras—he put his memoir on hold. He decided there was a more pressing topic that needed to be addressed, one that apparently had been brewing in his thoughts for years.

Even though his late-1970s operation of mixing-herbs-in-the-kitchen grew to a full-fledged business, with offices and a client database in New York by the mid-1980s, opposition to Dr. Sebi's natural healing practice loomed large. It came from a public reliant on conventional medicine and health insurance that covers it, from some churchgoers reluctant to embrace his

INTRODUCTION

sandal-wearing Afrocentric persona and style, and from politicians' standoffish position on the method he used to heal people.

In *Dr. Sebi Speaks of Dembali: Crossing Over from Dis-Ease to Ease in Matters of Health, Race, Family, and Culture*, he shows us the origin of the rejection and doubts and how to embrace truth. He called this process, which this book takes as its main subject, *dembali*. Dembali, according to Dr. Sebi, encompasses the reasons people reject recommendations that are beneficial to their lives in matters of health, race, family, and culture, even when evidence clearly shows that acceptance would be valuable and highly effective.

He intended to open eyes to dembali, to spark purpose-driven dialogue and reflection about our disconnection from the "cosmic arrangement of life" and how that separation prevents healing and genuine self-love—a separation that ushers in the rejection of something beneficial.

With *The Cure* on hold, I returned to Honduras in 2008 to help Dr. Sebi craft this book about dembali. He chose Roatán, Honduras, an island surrounded by the crystal-clear Caribbean Sea, as a perfect place to brainstorm, dictate, and write. Paya Bay Resort, our residence, gave us serene seclusion from busier parts of the island. Other than Dr. Sebi and me, the Paya Bay staff, and one other couple from the States, only an iguana or two passed by. Chapter Seven sheds light on that experience.

Passages in *Dr. Sebi Speaks of Dembali*, including those dembali-themed sections from the 2005 visit that were never published, are conversations I had with Dr. Sebi. They reveal—in a kind of fireside-chat setting—Dr. Sebi's feelings about and observations of people rejecting the good that his healing brings. These diamonds-in-the-rough can now break through the surface, shine, and take shape in the hearts and thoughts of others, and not solely black people. His views will resonate with all races. Health, malnutrition, self-sufficiency, love, hate, and culture are universal matters. They carry just as much weight and relevance today as they did when Dr. Sebi came on the scene over forty years ago. They still matter. Take the case of HIV/AIDS and the current buzz about the availability of medication, side effects associated with it, and the long-standing belief that there is no cure for the virus. Dr. Sebi's take on that hot topic is found in Chapter One, Section 2—His Work, "Natural Healing on Trial." He says,

> This book is written to show the world that what is going to happen is going to happen regardless, but this is the outcome of that particular journey. And they will put in the book the diagnostic sheets about AIDS. Meaning that will be the only thing in the book to show the world, yes, we cure AIDS. Well, if we could cure AIDS, what disease is there that is as devastating as AIDS? None.

The conversations are predecessors to the Black Lives Matter movement, steeped in Dr. Sebi's dembali and his opinion that if you know from whence you've come, you can overcome. For instance, he was unafraid to identify as an African man born in Honduras yet connected to an African resonance, a preslavery, precolonial sense of place and adherence to a life set by nature. Dr. Sebi considered African resonance a cosmic vibration or energy, one he tapped to help his natural healing methods succeed.

"I am today what I was yesterday, a bit adulterated…So, in the adulteration of my cells, I still remain hooked to that continent from whence I was taken away," Dr. Sebi said in Chapter Five.

He projected a strong constitution when he spoke at home. He was raw, frank—not a surprise or shock to some readers

INTRODUCTION

who knew him firsthand through friendship, public lectures, or browsing the internet. His awareness of and empathy with the black experience and psyche were sharp. I witnessed 360 degrees of it that week in November 2005 and again in September 2008. He shared his prognoses, his prescriptions, his adherence to the cosmic arrangement of life—an arrangement he called common-sense living, and a mindset that includes the complexities of sex. Yes, Dr. Sebi, an uninhibited man in conversations about the act and the genders, told me the whole world emerged from the "orifice of a vagina," so why not discuss it, revere it, and protect the owner of that prized organ (Chapter One)? We see that common-sense layer in his view of history and change, especially when it comes to race, health, family, and culture.

Dembali weaves its way through those insightful, and at times, edgy moments when he unleashed a verbal spanking on all of us (Chapter Four). You'll find dembali in Chapter One, where Dr. Sebi talks about a time in Washington, D.C., when incensed doctors found out he gave his herbal compounds to one of their patients, a young girl with sickle cell anemia.

I watched him roar—that passion and love in action—when he mentioned how people dismiss the connection between food and disease, throw their fates to the wind, then turn to him for healing. He obliged, of course. Dr. Sebi knew firsthand the struggle to change generational habits around the consumption of food and medicine. The source of the habits and the effects on emotions and behavior, particularly in black communities, are major themes in this book. Bear in mind, you'll find no sugarcoating in this story. Cards are laid out on the table for the whole world to see. But try to refrain from an urge to skip ahead or skim paragraphs to avoid unpleasant truths. Healing weaves its way through every word, every expletive, every fiery emotion, every rap on the knuckles. It's family conference at the dinner table time. And that's the way Dr. Sebi wanted it. He consistently expressed to me that for far too long black communities and the world at large buried liberating truths like the mythical ostrich head in the sand, while the fluffy feathers of indifference, impatience, and misunderstanding fluttered above in the wind. Dr. Sebi sits at the head of the table and reverses that trend in *Dr. Sebi Speaks of Dembali*.

Nonetheless, the autobiographical seeps through the pages, such as Dr. Sebi's relationship with his boyhood friends, who called him Fred or his nickname, Mama Hay, when they were growing up in Honduras. When he was a youngster, Dr. Sebi often accompanied his grandmother around the town of La Ceiba, prompting his friends to shout out the greeting, "Hey, Mama Hay!" The nickname stuck.

In La Ceiba, seated beneath a tree with a low canopy of leaves on a warm sunny afternoon, a group of seventy-year-olds ribbed each other about who was the oldest, played the card game Casino, and recounted memories of Fred and Mama Hay, his guardian from adolescence to adulthood (Chapter One).

But rest assured, ribbing and roars aside, Dr. Sebi loved us and wanted us to get our acts together. Straighten up and fly right, so to speak—health-wise, race-wise, family-wise, and culturally. He wanted us to return to the forest and heal.

Dr. Sebi Speaks of Dembali is arranged by topic: Dr. Sebi's biography and his work, as well as race, culture, identity, food, and the cosmic arrangement of life. And while together they represent a work of nonfiction, they read like short stories. Chapters begin

INTRODUCTION

with a narrative that previews the mood, people, location, and climate of each group of conversations. The table of contents hints at stories to come. Chapter One, "Black Women Encourage His Healing Journey," refers to black women who attended Dr. Sebi's house parties in the 1970s and opened his eyes to the world of herbs and natural living. They focused on imparting a social and cultural consciousness in their communities. As a matter of fact, these are the same women, actress Abby Lincoln included, who bestowed Alfredo Bowman with the name "Sebi, ever wandering traveler," in a naming ceremony. Dembali shadows this entire passage. But before we get there, let's recap Dr. Sebi's life.

The 1929 stock market crash in the United States ushered in the Great Depression. It affected the entire Western world's economy until the late 1930s. Even Latin American countries suffered, including Honduras, where the crisis hit hard. Banana exports, the lifeblood of the country's economy, pretty much dwindled to a halt. Dr. Sebi was born in Honduras during that scant period.

On November 26, 1933, he descended from the warmth of Violet's womb in a rural area called Ilanga. Violet named her son—her third child—Alfredo Darrington Bowman. He was born to a race of people called Black Caribs or Garifuna, Africans brought to Honduras and the Caribbean by British colonists in the 1600s. Garifunas represented approximately 2 percent of the Honduran population in the 1930s. Today, around three hundred thousand Garifunas, who also embrace the title Afro-Honduran, live in Honduras, Belize, and Guatemala.

Violet took care of Alfredo for the first eight years of his life and then sent him to the coastal city of La Ceiba to live with her mother, the resilient Ann Hay. She raised Alfredo for ten years in this economically challenged climate. Alfredo affectionately called his grandmother Mama Hay. When he recalled his family's history, he said,

> Mama Hay is a young lady that was born in Belize. She was born in the Protectorate, the Principality of Belize under the British at the time. About her life with her mother, I know very little. I know a lot about her life with her grandmother, Elizabeth, my great-great-grandmother. And according to my grandmother she was a very tall woman, very strong woman. She lived until the age of 124. Then my grandmother, Mama Hay, was born to Carolina. Carolina had two girls. Mama Hay was one. I don't remember the name of the other girl. Mama Hay grew up very attached to her mother...So, I am a product of these four black women—Violet, Mama Hay, Carolina, and Elizabeth. I resonate with these women.

Mama Hay lived long enough to see her grandson become a merchant seaman and travel around the world on cargo ships, but passed away before he became an accomplished natural healer. "I was blessed to have Mama Hay, who demanded nothing but integrity of me at all times."

Alfredo settled down in a US city his cargo ship sailed to often—New Orleans. He lost his virginity there with an obliging Barbara Diggs. He would have married her, but his twenty-one-plus days at sea put a damper on that. Barbara favored a landlocked relationship, one she eventually found with another man. Alfredo understood and moved on too.

INTRODUCTION

Influenced by his grandmother's teachings of self-reliance and her stories about Marcus Garvey, leader of the Back to Africa movement, Alfredo joined the Nation of Islam in New Orleans in the 1950s. He helped its members' businesses serve Negro communities when Jim Crow laws were the order of the day. Shortly afterward, he traveled to Chicago to meet its leader, Elijah Muhammad and chief spokesperson Malcolm X. Around the same time, he married and started his first family. His wife, Melba, bore three sons—Alfredo Bowman Jr., Clifford, and Abdul—and one daughter, Jamala. But in 1964, Alfredo experienced two critical events: Clifford's death from a respiratory illness and the rift between Elijah Muhammad and Malcolm X, an irreversible falling out that caused division within and exodus from the Nation of Islam. Alfredo held onto his rock-solid support of Malcolm and joined the exit. He moved his family to Los Angeles, where, in 1970, he received employment at Martin Luther King Jr./Drew Medical Center and worked there for ten years as a thermal engineer.

Before his journey to heal others, Alfredo's own illnesses—impotence, diabetes, and obesity—were cured thanks to a friend who recommended that he go to Mexico to see an herbalist. Alfredo agreed. He traveled to Mexico with a conviction that he would abide by the Mexican's treatments since all others had failed him. After ninety days of taking the herbs, Alfredo's diseases disappeared. Encouraged by his recovery, he conducted experiments with water and natural plants such as cascara sagrada and chaparral. Friends suffering from various ailments gave him permission to administer these herbal mixtures to them. Removing diseases like diabetes and lowering high blood pressure inspired him to delve deeper into the research of herbal compounds and remedies for other ailments. By 1980 this had become a full-time passion and career. He parlayed the mother wit inherited from

Mama Hay and encouragement from friends in Los Angeles into a commitment to use alkaline herbs and plants to heal people.

He traveled to the Caribbean, Mexico, and Africa for research and to collect herbs. He embraced the name "Sebi," called his herbal compounds the African Bio Mineral Balance, and watched his mom-and-pop operation blossom into a full-fledged natural healthcare business called The Fig Tree, operated by his Usha Herbal Research Institute. Clients who suffered from cancer, diabetes, lupus, sickle cell anemia, and AIDS were treated and cured. (Yes, cured. Documents can attest to that fact.) Awestruck laypeople who witnessed his success immediately bestowed the title "doctor" upon him. Sebi accepted it and thereafter was known as Dr. Sebi.

With a public speaking tour in full swing in the 1980s, he shared his healing method and products with captivated audiences from southeastern United States to New York. At a private home in Washington, D.C., a journalist from Howard University's radio station WHUR also decided to ride the wave with Dr. Sebi. She sat in the audience with other colleagues from the station. By the time Dr. Sebi ended his talk, the journalist knew she wanted to share his work with listeners of WHUR's public affairs program *The Sunday Digest*. I invited him to the station. He agreed to come. The rest, as they say, is history.

Dr. Sebi faced a host of challenges as a natural healer, including razor-sharp scrutiny by the New York attorney general's office. It brought The Fig Tree before the New York Supreme Court and the US Food and Drug Administration. Yet years after his victory in court, and four years after his death, the public continues to seek Dr. Sebi's products and the nutritional guidance he imparted to generations. I count myself as one of them. Dr. Sebi's African Bio Mineral Balance products have been mainstays in my life since I met him over two decades ago.

"And this is why for us to really get over, get over meaning what, from the state of disease to ease, that jump, that crossing over is called dembali."

Dr. Sebi, November 2005

Dis-Ease

Black, Latino patients much more likely than whites to undergo amputations related to diabetes
Source: Anna Gorman, CNN, Kaiser Permanente News

On his regular rounds at the University of Southern California's Keck Hospital, Dr. David Armstrong lives a brutal injustice of American health care. Each week, dozens of patients with diabetes come to him with deep wounds, severe infections and poor circulation—debilitating complications of a disease that has spiraled out of control... In California, where doctors performed more than 82,000 diabetic amputations from 2011 to 2017, people who were black or Latino were more than twice as likely as non-Hispanic whites to undergo amputations related to diabetes, a Kaiser Health News analysis found.

Ease

Chapter 6: Starch, A 400-Year Consumption
Source: Dr. Sebi, *Sojourn to Honduras Sojourn to Healing*

A sister was treated in San Diego, California. They were about to remove both of her feet. And we gave her the compounds and she recovered. But we told her not to eat the bean pie because the bean pie was too high in glucose and it affected her. She had diabetes. Her feet were black. She has a picture of it. Her name is Sister Paula. She was told by us to discontinue eating lamb or beef or chicken because her blood was septic. To remove the condition and save her, we recommended that she had to stop eating those things...When she stopped, they called it a miracle. They called it a miracle. The woman has both of her feet. They didn't have to remove them, amputate her feet, and she does not have diabetes.

CHAPTER ONE

From the Rainforest to the USA

Section 1—Biography

Alfredo, the River, and the Rain

I stay in Honduras from November 6 through 12, 2005, Sunday through Saturday. It's a warm, hurricane-recovering autumn. In early October Hurricane Stan struck Central America, leaving $1.5 billion in damages behind. Merciless downpours continued into late October when Hurricane Wilma's rainstorms and high wind force, thrashing at over one hundred miles per hour, swept across a region already flooded by Stan. Surprisingly, I see only a few signs of either one when I arrive at Usha: a few palm leaves thrown about and thin metal roofs on the ground. A mound of debris lies in a corner beside the woods that surround the property's hot spring.

Morning in the tropics—anytime between five and nine, when shiny palm leaves have recovered from a raucous night of steady rain or when temperatures are less sweat-inducing than the ninety-degree afternoons—is the ideal time for recorded conversations with Sebi. Low humidity. Crickets barely awake. Warblers, parakeets, and thick-billed seed finches call out from mango tree branches at Usha Village. Sebi has been up since four o'clock watching the international news or a game that lifts him forward and off his pillows a bit—soccer.

"Why should it be difficult to remember three years of age?" Sebi asks in our first interview of the week. It's a Monday morning. "I remember when I was four. When I was four, it was the only time I experienced fear for a minute."

"When you were four?" I repeat, to make sure I'm clear about milestones and events in his childhood that shaped the man he would become, a man who speaks of dembali.

"Yeah. Because everybody left my mother and I just alone on this wagon. And my mother told me years later, forty years later, that they were running after a jaguar."

"How about that log story? That sounds so farfetched. You were in the water? So you followed the shrimp into the river?"

"Into the deeper part," he recounts.

"And you didn't realize you were going deeper and deeper into it. How did you get there? You were a little boy at the time."

"Yeah, I was three."

"And you didn't realize it."

"I didn't. I used to go to the river every day. And you know, I went back to that place fifty years later. I went back fifty-six years later, and I asked the lady, the first time I went back to Ilanga, and I asked the woman that was standing there. I said,

'Lady, I haven't been to Ilanga in fifty-seven years. I want to ask you a question. If I take this road here, would I go straight to the river?'

She said, 'Yeah. How do you know that?'

I said, 'Because I remember certain things about Ilanga. I want to ask you another question. How old are you?' She said she was sixty-four or fifty-seven or something, but she was two years older than me.

I said, 'Well, you should know 'cause you didn't leave this place.'

She said, 'No.'

I said, 'Do you remember a woman who used to live right there on the corner that takes a Y?'

She said, 'Yes, it was a black woman. I never really know her name.'

I said, 'That's my momma. Were there seven houses here?'

'No, there were nine.'

But I remember that. I was two houses off. Yeah, there were nine. I remember seven."

"You have a great memory, especially going back to three years old," I say.

"Oh girl, that's easy." He shrugs it off.

I don't think so. I visualize a tiny child struggling for dear life, gasping for breath as water fills his mouth. "So you grabbed on. I want to hear that story some more. So you grabbed hold of the logs."

"Yeah, and the logs were turning around, but finally one of the logs spinned around, and the point of it was heading towards the shallow part. And I was able to get out. And when I got home I was wet. I was frightened. I was frightened, like, yeah, I got away from something bad." He chuckles. "And my momma didn't know until this day why I got home wet."

"You must have been a real strong three-year-old," I say, amazed at his resilience.

"I wasn't strong. How could a little three-year-old be strong?" he asks, modestly brushing off the compliment.

"Well, you held on tight. You didn't let go."

"I was struggling for life like everybody would have done."

"Right, but some people probably would just say well, let me just turn loose."

"Turn loose?" he wisecracks, as if I should know better than to attach that idea to him.

"Yeah."

"Girl, I ain't turn loose ever in my life on anything."

I laugh. That statement laid the foundation for conversations to come.

"Hold on," Sebi repeats.

"Right. Hold on. Yeah, that's good," I say, wrapped in the flow of this mellow moment.

"I'll hold on," he says again with a chuckle.

Ready to talk about the source of his tenacity, I ask him about family members he mentioned in his autobiography, *The Cure*—his mother Violet and his grandmother Mama Hay, women who raised him during a lean time in Honduras.

"Evidently, it must have been good because I didn't go to school either, and here I am curing AIDS. I'm curing sickle cell anemia. How did that happen? It happened out of the environment provided for me by my grandmother."

"Your grandmother and great-grandmother. So they prepared the way for you to do what you're doing?"

"They did."

"That's divine order," I say out of the blue, an impulsive statement that pushes our conversation into a totally different realm.

"Everything is in divine order, including Hitler. Wasn't he in divine order?"

"Yes," I agree slowly.

"Well, how did he exist if it wasn't in divine order?"

We've reached an instructor-student phase of the conversation. Sebi speaks as if he's standing in front of a classroom full of students. "Yes, divine order. I believe that," I say.

"No. It's not a belief," Sebi instructs. "You cannot write history of a hundred years hence without including Hitler, whether you want to or not. He existed. That is the reality I am talking about. Everything is in divine order. You and ants, Hitler, a duck. Everything is in divine order. So my grandmother," he says, pulling us back into the subject at hand, "yeah, my grandmother Mama Hay—"

"Mama Hay, is that her real name?" I ask.

"Her name was Ann Hay. But they call her Mama Hay because she took on that persona only because she used to play these cards. And I used to wonder why this woman play these cards. And I remember they were those tarot cards. And people used to come with tears in their eyes, and they used to leave smiling."

Though severed from his body like a butterfly's fallen cocoon, Sebi's umbilical cord imbued him with the essence of Mama Hay and three other strong women of meager means, yet resolute, nonetheless. They included his mother Violet, born in Honduras; his grandmother Mama Hay, born in Belize; his great-grandmother Carolina, born in Jamaica; and his great-great-grandmother Elizabeth, born in Belize.

"The great-great-grandmother, the baddest one of them

all," Sebi boasts, one of the rare times he does. "The one that my mother will tell you about. My grandmother remembers her, of the flood of 1919, 1920. No. My mother was nine." He pauses to recollect the history. "My mother was born in 1916, the flood of 1925. This tall black woman held onto my mother on this post in the flood. She was a strong woman, and she was already in her hundreds. Oh yeah. So you see, I'm happy. I'm happy that I'm a recipient of that gene. People on my father's side, they die young. Not on my mother's side. No, they live long. So I now have given you a history that I received from my mother and from my grandmother. So, we're going to visit my mother and let her talk about her mother, which is my grandmother that raised me. But she can talk about her great-grandmother, which is Elizabeth."

"Really?"

"Oh yes, definitely. And when Mama Hay left Belize, Mama Hay left Belize at the age of thirty. When she went back to Belize, my grandmother was eighty-five years old. So fifty-five years had gone by. She had not seen her mother in fifty-five years. So I asked her, I said, 'What you going back to Belize for?'"

'To see my mother,' she said.

"I teased her. I said, 'Grandmother you crazy.'"

'Oh yeah? I'm going back.'

"And my grandmother went back to Belize, and her mother was 109, 110. So fifty-five years had gone by. My great-grandmother went into the yard with my grandmother to tell her what happened the last fifty-five years that she was absent. My grandmother said she didn't come to hear that. She told her mother, 'I come to see you.' Golly, boy, this is two black women. I love the history of my grandparents because my grandmother is standing there telling this woman, her mother, that she didn't come to hear what happened in the last fifty years. 'I came to see you.' And then they got down to talk about other things. And then my great-grandmother told my grandmother, 'When you hear that I have passed you laugh, because I have been waiting for you. It is you I was waiting for.' When my grandmother board that boat to come back from Belize, on the way to Honduras, the captain told my grandmother, 'Your mother just passed.' So when I came to Honduras, my grandmother told me the same thing. 'When you hear that I have passed don't you cry. You're going to laugh.' And I did that. So the richness was instilled in the family. It was part of these women. It wasn't that they learned it. It was in 'em. It resonated in 'em. And by me being raised by one of these women, I saw and I received from that vibration. And this is what I put into motion. Mama Hay son, which is Lucius, said to my mother when he was only nine years of age, 'I would never work for anybody. I would never work for any man as long as I live.' And he didn't."

"Never?"

"Never. And he became a furniture maker. The tuck-and-weave was his stuff. In fact, he got a patent or two or three or four. Yes, he never worked for any man. He owned the factory. Like my brother son said, 'I'm not going to work for anyone.' And he didn't. He owns an airline. So you see, it's easy for us. But for an American, it's a hell of an accomplishment, when it is not. It isn't. You do it."

I hear the pride in his voice. His family's affinity for self-reliance and independence surfaced, so I probe his history further. "Now, what about Violet? What was Violet like? You were with her from the time you were born until eight when you went to live with Mama Hay. What were the eight years like?"

"Oh, they were beautiful. I remember they were beautiful. I remember as far back as one and a half I could remember my mother, not to mention when I was four, when we were taken away from Ilanga to go to Planes. And we were going across this plain on this wagon pulled by a bulldozer. And I remember everybody leaving."

"That's the jaguar story," I say. I remembered reading about it in the manuscript of his memoir.

"And then I remember being with her, seeing her bake and me standing by the table waiting for her to make a small little cookie for me. I was five. I remember many things of my mother. And then I remember her bringing me to La Ceiba, or taking me to La Ceiba from Planes to my grandmother. But it was good, all the way, because it was the way it was supposed to be. And I enjoyed it because I was a child."

"Why did she do that? Why did she let your grandmother take care of you?"

"Well, because in Latin America, unlike America, it's a privilege for the woman to give the child to the grandmother," he says with a chuckle, "because she is the grandmother. The mother knows the grandmother is going to perform a better job than she can."

In all our conversations, from 2005 until our last one in 2015, Sebi never said a negative word about his relationship with his mother or grandmother. He spoke highly of both of them—always. But I sensed there may have been a somber reason that Violet sent her son and none of her other children to live with Mama Hay. Lack of resources? The world was still reeling from the Depression. A rift with his stepfather? Sebi rarely talked about him.

"Now, Violet Francis, your mom, you told a very, very moving story about when she was sick. Describe that whole ordeal, when she was sick and you were underneath the—"

"the floor"

"And it was raining. How did she get sick?"

"Well, I didn't know. I was only five," he says. "That was in Planes, and I was already five. And she was sick. And we were living under this floor. And I said I would like to help my mother one day, that she would never get sick, that I could heal her. But I didn't know that out of that, at five, that I would be doing for the whole world. But it was a statement."

I notice all of Sebi's statements about his grandmothers and women in general are heartfelt. His usual robust Yul Brynneresque voice lowers to a mellow tone of respect and joy when he speaks about them. But his paternal grandmother Sarah Phillips, a brothel owner in La Ceiba, holds a different place in his heart.

"You said you lived with her for about a year. You were seven years old, right?"

"Well, I don't think it was a year, really. I said that because I remember living with her but I don't think it was a year, no. It wasn't a year. It wasn't even a month, I think. Because, see, I remember doing something that irritated her. I used to pee in the bed every night."

"Oh. By mistake? Was it a mistake?"

"Hell no."

"On purpose?"

"Straight. I didn't want to be there. I piss in the bed."

"So they took you there. Who took you there, your mother, Violet?"

"No. My aunt wanted me to be with the father's side of the family for a little while." Sebi was six months old when someone murdered his father, Clifford Bowman.

"Oh, I see, I see, just as a visit, a get-acquainted visit but you didn't want to be there."

"How could I feel that? I couldn't feel that. I felt Mama Hay. Yeah," he says, defending his love for her. "Hey, everything in my life, you know, like when I left Honduras, I looked at that red light, the last thing I saw, I thought about Mama Hay, that I was leaving her. Yeah."

"Do you have regrets about leaving?"

"No, I had to. I didn't have no regrets, because if I had regrets I wouldn't have left. No regrets."

"It was just a calling to go."

"It was a calling to go."

On Our Way to La Ceiba

Groundskeepers arrive and put in a few hours of digging and dredging dirt and trimming bushes to pretty up Usha. They clean up the leaves, branches, and debris Hurricane Wilma's rainstorms flung across the village two weeks earlier. Shortly after the men finish, Sebi's ready to look things over before we take a ride to La Ceiba.

He says, "Wait, because I want two entrances."

He gets out of the truck to talk to one of his groundskeepers. His wife, Matun, and I watch from inside Sebi's mini truck while he inspects and commends the work like a proud papa. On his twenty-acre property, birds flutter by from mango trees to almond trees, then back to the mangoes. I hear faint sounds of vehicles driving past Usha's entrance, about two blocks down the driveway. Sebi returns to the truck and updates us about his goals for the center.

"Yeah, girl," he says, then he addresses Matun. "This right here, baby, this is going to be a beautiful little sitting area, right there. And this is going to be the aquatic garden, right here."

The mini truck's windows are down. Passing cars and the truck's engine nearly drown out the conversation inside the truck. Every other mile or so, Sebi steers the vehicle down a stretch of graveled road. Bumps and jolts in the back seat jerk the microphone and tape recorder I try to hold steady. When the terrain and mood inside the truck smooth out, Sebi drives up and speaks Spanish to La Ceiba police, his comrades in civil service. One of them about to receive a dose of Sebi's generosity.

La Ceiba Police 1: Doctor!

Sebi: Hable usted al maestro!

La Ceiba Police 1: No, somos dos

La Ceiba Police 2: dijo que la dejara

Sebi: Esto es importante, esto es muy importante. Digale que va a tomar 4 en la manana y 4 en la tarde. Que es importante

Sebi asks for the boss and is told he's not in. He leaves an herbal compound along with instructions on dosage with the police officer. He tells him that the compound sells for fifty dollars in the US, but there is no charge for the boss. What a treat to hear Sebi speak in his native language. I've heard black people speak African languages and Caribbean patois, never fluent Spanish. "That's the police department?" I ask.

"Yep," Sebi and Matun answer.

"They're the cops," he says. "I meet with the cops. I'm a cop myself."

After all he had been through with them, he joined them anyway. "You're a cop?"

"Yeah. I meet with the auxiliary police. My job going to begin in January 1 to clean up this sector. And any time we find a piece of trash, everybody that live in that sector will be paying a fine, a very heavy fine, regardless to how small the trash is, a piece of paper or whatever, you gonna pay. See, like it's clean here, right?"

"Yes," I say, noticing the litter-free road as Sebi drives by.

"Well, it's gonna stay like that. And we're not going to play. And any bus that we see people throwing things out, the bus is going to pay a fine of 1500 lempiras."

His job has already begun it seems. His voice takes on a dutiful and authoritarian tone.

"You have to clean it up. And the government gave me the okay, so I'll begin to exercise my civil powers. Honduras is a pretty country."

"It is beautiful," I agree wholeheartedly.

"We're gonna take you to the Maya ruins. There's beauty all around. You're looking at it."

I mention his other house up in the mountains, which brings a thrill to him.

"Ah, now, that's a horse of a different color."

"Now, the one that's there now, can you look down and see the water?"

"The one at Sambo Creek right here up on the hill?" he asks.

"Yes."

"You can see the water, 180 degrees. That's all you see. You can even see the islands, hey baby?" he asks Matun.

"Um-hm. It's a panoramic view," Matun adds.

And it doesn't cost much for that panoramic view of the Caribbean. Sebi informs me retired people from the United States can save a lot of money living in Honduras because real estate is far cheaper than in North America. Rent or mortgage for a three-bedroom house is around $500 per month. We ride past housing construction. At first glance it resembles housing developments you'd see in the US, some more complete than others. We ride farther along, beside the base of high, lush mountains.

"Now, what do the tourists do when they come here Sebi?" I ask him, taking in expansive views of the countryside.

"What tourists?"

"Oh, no tourists, oh okay."

"Well, I don't handle tourists. I handle sick people. Yeah. I don't deal with tourists. They go to the mountain. They go hiking. But the tourists go to Utila because Honduras is next to the Great Barrier Reef. We're the second."

"Have we passed any of the banana farms yet?"

"No, we're not even close to them. They're behind those mountains," he points out.

Since he's joined the ranks of civil servants, I steer the conversation toward politics. "Who is the president of Honduras or the prime minister or, what do you call him?"

"The president," he says.

"His name?"

"I don't know."

I'm shocked to hear this. He's one of the most politically savvy people I know. "You don't know who the president is, Sebi, of your hometown?" Before he answers there's a pause.

"I don't know his name. You see, those are the things you haven't learned about Sebi. I don't know the president name because I don't know his name. I must have learned something, right?"

"Uh-huh." Matun defends him.

"What, what did I lose?"

"No, you didn't lose anything, no, no, no, for not knowing," I say.

"I don't know his name. I don't know a whole lot of presidents' name. I know Mugabe because I've been to his country. I know Sahko. I don't know nobody else."

That's not entirely true. If our subject that week had been botany, history, science, or social studies, he would have rambled facts, names, and places as well as any doctoral student.

"What are the things in life that are important to you Sebi? What's important?" I ask.

"What's important to Sebi? There was never anything. I can't single out an item. Can you single out an item that's important to you? Well, I can't either."

"It seems like you get high, you get like this blissful feeling about the herbs and healing. I mean, you say that healing is the least of what you can do, like curing AIDS is the least of what you can do. But whenever you talk about the herbs and plants and nature, boy do you light up, brighten up, get excited. So those things are important to you, right?" He greets a passerby before he answers.

"Señor! Saluda! Another cop. See all these cops. Po-leese. But they know Dr. Sebi. 'So it's amazing! You didn't give energy to anything Dr. Sebi?'" he continues. "No."

"Yeah, it's divine order," I say. "You're where you're supposed to be."

"That must be me because I'm always with you," Matun interjects, noting her contribution to Sebi's life. The three of us laugh.

"I think she's right. You are my god," Sebi says.

"Goddess," I joke.

The sensual steps in. Sebi's boyish when he reveals he appreciates and accepts a woman's sexuality, an uninhibited sexuality. Some of the remarks are tongue-in-cheek, but I wonder if I should stop recording. I'm usually awed by Sebi's wisdom and his success in natural healing. Now I sit shy and blush at his frank sex talk. He taunts me, asks me why my illustrious Dr. Sebi can speak truth about disease, food, herbs, and healing but stay close-lipped when it comes to sex. The tape recorder rolls on.

"She's my god and everything else," he says in a melodious tone. "She's a woman. She's a black woman that I will forever need. I will forever need. I'm indebted to her. Mama Hay told me any man that spends his life complimenting woman, he's happy all his life. Any man that opposes woman, he's angry all his life. Well, I chose the prior. I chose to be a slave to woman. And I love it because they love it too, yes. And you know they could sense my acceptance of the totality of the woman, you know. They take all kinds of privileges with me. They tell me all kinds of things. All that they do to poor old Sebi. Boy, the healer have to go through all kinds of stuff to remind him you're a human being. You came through a vagina. We can put it in your face. If you object, we want to know why. Yeah, we want to know why, Sebi. You call yourself having understanding. Well, didn't you come through the orifice of a vagina? That's the kind of woman I attract to Dr. Sebi. I know you're going to write that," he quips.

"Well, not all of it," I wince. If I were two shades lighter, I'd be red in the face.

"Well, you better write all of it, because that's the way it was said," he teases.

"Okay. Haven't you ever heard of a thing called editing?"

"See, that's what's wrong with America."

"Ninety-nine point nine—"

"That's what's wrong with America," he interrupts.

"No," I reply.

"America is a country where you can't tell the truth."

"You're telling the truth but, Sebi, come on now." I chuckle some more.

"But see what? That's conjecture."

"We're going to put 99.9 percent of it in the book. But you're tickling me. You tickle me."

"Well you're not going to put it in the book that my wife put her vagina in my face?"

I shriek. Yes, I did. "Oh my God!"

"Oh, you're not going to put it in there?"

"I don't know. Oh, I just have to—oh, I don't know. I might have to get you to say it another way."

"Can't be truthful." He rests his case.

"You can be truthful," I assure him, but I'm clearly losing the debate.

"No, you can't. No, no, no, you cannot be truthful."

"This book is going out to the world."

"Eh, to what?" he asks, in a tone of quirkiness and surprise.

Matun chimes in. "The world came out of a vagina."

"The whole world came through a vagina," Sebi concurs.

"I know. I know," I say, still blushing and running out of logical reasons to leave this conversation out of the book.

"All right. But you got to talk about these things because it's forbidden," he continues gently.

"It's private," Matun adds.

"Oh yeah? Well, who forbid it?" Sebi asks playfully. "Who is the one that put this top on it and this lid? Me, um-m-m-m, bring on the wickedness."

"Sweet nectar, huh?" I join in.

"Bring on the iniquity and the wickedness," he singsongs.

I had reservations about revealing this conversation. I felt some readers might prefer that Sebi's private pleasures were best left private. But I let those doubts go. I decided I would not wimp out and let editors determine if the material should stay in or stay out. I find it healthy, and to a large degree, liberating, to know and share Sebi's feelings about the vagina at a time when women and babies around the world suffer the ravages of genital mutilation at the behest of men. The World Health Organization reports over 200 million girls and women have been cut.[1] Many experienced severe bleeding, problems urinating, and later cysts, infections, and complications in childbirth. Female genital mutilation is an age-old tradition in Africa, Asia, and the Middle East. But it's one Sebi, a traditionalist, would oppose. The subject never came up in our conversations but I'm confident that Sebi opposed female circumcision.

"I want you to put this one in the book." He leads us into another lighthearted moment from his past. "This is Dr. Reverend Albert Brooks, who is head of the Episcopal Church here in Honduras. He is the man that told me, 'Yeah, here comes the devil. Look at him, the devil himself. Yeah, you may have good tidings. Well, I'm going to tell you the good tidings are from God, devil.' Boy, I like that. I be liking Albert. Albert, oh Albert. I love Albert. Albert could look at me and see that I am the devil." He chuckles.

Suddenly, while we're still riding around La Ceiba, Sebi observes a traffic jam up ahead. Apparently, a driver wants to change lanes in bumper to bumper lines of vehicles. Sebi's courtesy kicks in. I ask him why he's shaking his head at this incident.

"Because there's a language in Honduras—"

"Yeah," Matun says. She notices too.

"The same language exists in Puerto Rico. You understand?"

I ask him what it is.

"The same language exists in Puerto Rico, that when you see a man in trouble, and you see. Come on, man. You know you cool. You know, you let him go."

I notice Sebi's down-to-earth civility in this incident.

"That's Latin America. You're in the right of way. But he needs to get in. So you let him in. How much did it cost you? It didn't cost you anything."

Our afternoon excursion around the city of La Ceiba continues. I witness Sebi's generosity once again. He drives down the road in twenty-miles-per-hour traffic and stops in a quaint community of shotgun houses. A small group of family and friends runs out. They cheer and surround him as if a revered king has just arrived. Efaywah and Rudy live in this little town. They're friends of Sebi's ten-year-old daughter, Saama. I met all of them my first day at Usha.

Sebi shouts, "Efaywah!"

With the little Spanish I know, I greet her too. "Efaywah, hi. ¿Cómo estás?"

I sit on the edge of the back seat, smiling out the window at all the excitement and gift-giving, including a cell phone for a friend who asked Sebi for one. Before she comes to the truck to get it, a girl around seven years old greets Sebi and gestures to see the phone. Matun joins the camaraderie. She speaks Spanish to the little girl, asking her if she likes the phone. She does. When the lady comes to the truck to get it, Sebi says,

"Solo tiend que esperar dos horas para que te lo activen." (You only have to wait two hours for it to be activated.)

"Yap ague para todo, ese es tu telefono que querias." (I already paid for everything. That's the phone that you wanted.)

Gently, the lady replies, "Gracias."

Alfredo's Birth Bed

Sebi, Matun, and I arrive at the home of Sebi's ninety-year-old mother, Violet Francis. Her pregnant granddaughter Cosi, who appears to be in her early thirties, is cooking in the kitchen nearby.

Ms. Francis grew up in the rural hills of Honduras during the first two decades of the twentieth century. She lived in the bush, the deep bush, surviving in an environment that required her family to make do with the resources it provided, unlike other black Hondurans who eked out a living in town or near the coast. Now she lives in a modest but comfortable house in La Ceiba.

When we walk through the door, Ms. Francis is watching television in the living room. She sits upright and relaxed with her legs propped up in a leather recliner. I imagine that if she were standing, she would be as tall as Sebi, but stouter. She wears a pink and burgundy kaftan, while white, fluffy bedroom slippers cover her feet. Her cornrow-styled gray braids drape the nape of her neck. They allow a clear view of a face that flashes, "I am Dr. Sebi's mother." Even with her eyeglasses on, the lineage is undeniable. I'm awed and grateful for the privilege to share this space with a woman whose resilience and tenacity as a young mother helped her raise a son who not only opened our eyes to the root of disease, but gave us remedies we could use.

Looking around her home, I can tell Ms. Francis likes nice things. Next to her in the living room stands a brown, backless wooden bookcase, with four shelves in three sections, that serves as a divider between the kitchen and the living room. The shelf second from the top holds lightweight matching lanterns that sit across from a set of two shiny navy-blue vases with handles, each about eight inches tall. The shelf below displays framed family photos in various sizes, a few black and white, the majority in color, all tightly lined up across the bookcase's three sections. The wall behind Ms. Francis holds a vintage mirror with a light goldish brown frame. A matching table with slender legs stands underneath it. Set on top of it is a dainty white ten-inch tall vase filled with pastel-colored artificial flowers.

"I'm glad that she's here because when she came to me with her body that was somewhat sick, she was seventy," Sebi says, when we start our visit with his mother.

"What did she have? Can you tell me?"

"The same thing every lady seventy that's never taken care of herself had: poor knees, poor circulation. She didn't have the high blood pressure," he shares.

"Fantastic."

"She didn't have sugar. She got both of her breasts. And that's cool because nowadays it's questionable after you pass fifty if you're going to have your breasts. And she sleeps on the bed that I was born on."

"She still sleeping in the bed that you were born on Dr. Sebi?" I blurt out.

"Yeah. Come see."

"Oh, I would love to. My goodness. This is a beautiful house." Needless to say, I'm ecstatic and honored to travel back in time to catch a glimpse of Sebi's past. I walk with a devotee's pace, but I'm like a child in a candy store when we enter his mother's bedroom.

"Sebi!" I shout. "This is where you were born?"

"She gave birth to me on this bed."

"On this bed—not in this house though, right?"

"In the jungle. In the forest."

"This is the bed," I repeat softly, spellbound by a sight that's comparable to laying eyes on God's throne.

"Um-hm," Sebi answers.

"And this is the mommy that you saved. This the mommy that was underneath the—"

"This is the woman."

I marvel at the fortitude of this black woman, who, like her three-year-old son fighting for his life in the Aguan River, held on through a downpour of water capable of ending life, a black woman who persevered in lean times and lived to see her son parlay water's power into a source of healing and strength. Her resolve to live provided the springboard for Alfredo Bowman to become the healer and influencer that stands before me. But, it's as if I'm seeing Sebi for the first time. Is this the same man in the YouTube videos? The public lectures? Physically yes, but in a familial sense, he's greater.

"Oh gosh Sebi. This is your bed," I gush out, awestruck by the heirloom.

"Um-hm. So, see, it's too soft now. We have to fix this because she wants to give it to me. That's too soft. And I'm gonna take it, because it's mine."

"Yes, this is a family heirloom."

"So, I have to change the whole thing. And it's a nice bed. I could have it straight and put the new—"

Matun enters the room and joins the conversation. "Does she want that mattress? She's comfortable with that?" she asks.

"She shouldn't be because that's too soft. And I'm gonna tell Marie I have to buy something better than that, something hard. Yeah that's too soft. And this, this here, so you say this bed here is how old?"

"Over seventy," I say.

"Seventy-two, seventy-four, seventy-five years old, approximately."

Truly a family heirloom I tell Sebi. He agrees. Matun fancies the curtains with pink flowers. I lay my eyes on a fine-looking rug and ask him where it came from.

"Mexico," he says, taking us back to the living room to continue our visit with his mother. Once there, Matun compliments Ms. Francis on her pretty room. It really is, with absolutely no sign of the hard times in Honduras.

"It's beautiful," I say. "Mrs. Bowman, right?"

Sebi says her last name is Francis. It had slipped my mind because up until our visit with her, the surname Bowman had filled my thoughts. "Ms. Francis, that's right. Ms. Francis, this is a beautiful home." She laughs softly.

"Here come the grandchildren," Sebi points out. "The great-grandchildren."

A four-year-old girl comes up to me. "Hi, how are you?"

"Fine, thank you. And you?" she says sweetly.

"Fine." I point her in the direction of Ms. Francis, her great-grandmother. "Who is that?"

"Hi, Grandma."

"Hi, how are you?" Ms. Francis replies.

"Fine, thank you. And you?"

"Good, thanks to the Lord."

I ask Sebi if Cosi is the little girl's mother. When he replies no, Cosi joins the conversation to help identify the relatives, which are many.

"Talk English?" Cosi asks. Sebi and Matun answer yes together.

"That's Noel daughter?" Sebi asks.

"Yeah," Cosi replies.

The little girl, Noel's daughter, is Sebi's grandniece. Noel is the son of Sebi's half-brother Felix Gale, a deceased pastor and father of ten children in La Ceiba, including Noel and Cosi.

"When Cosi was small," Sebi recalls, "Cosi did something that I will never forget. Cosi took the broom and she was about to slam her sister with this broom. And her daddy came to the window and said, 'What you expect to do?' 'Oh, I was going to sweep the floor.'" All of us laugh at Cosi's childhood mischief. "Boy, Cosi did that so fast. Boy, I said no way, no way," Sebi says with a chuckle. "Ah-h. I have to buy Cosi a birthday present. She's a Scorpio."

"Her birthday is coming up?" I ask.

"No, her birthday was the second of November. Her and Maxine are Scorpios."

Maxine is Sebi's sister—Violet's fourth child. She married and moved to Memphis, Tennessee. When her birthday and other family events and milestones have been shared, we wrap up our visit and start riding again.

I recap the visit. "Mama Hay's daughter."

"That's my girl," Sebi boasts.

"Your girl."

"That's my girlfriend."

"And she's a wonderful, beautiful girlfriend," I echo, still awed by meeting his mother.

"Badass woman, I'm gonna tell you that."

"So strong."

Matun adds that Ms. Francis makes the best tamales in the world. She even makes tamales and sends them by FedEx. That surprises me. But I learned on this trip to Sebi's native world that when a Bowman or Francis wants something done, they just do it, no matter what it takes.

"Vegetable tamales," Matun says, practically singing the praises. "Good, good, good."

"Vegetable tamales, what I had yesterday?" I ask.

"Something like that," Sebi and Matun say.

"You know," Sebi adds, "she made all these children and all of us. My brother Allen was a mechanic. He used to have a big mechanical shop, diesel and everything else. And my other brother was a preacher and a builder. John is a business owner. Myself, I turned out to be what I am, whatever that is. But she never expected to see all of that or anything because she don't live in that world. We don't live in that world. This is why the word 'future' was never in our vocabulary. The future? What future? Who has that? Those who believe in it. But we didn't believe in it. My mother just lived. She became a Christian in her late forties."

"Why did she become a Christian?" I ask, wondering if her deceased son Pastor Felix Gale influenced her.

"I don't know. I never asked her."

A Street Corner in La Ceiba

Our drive in Sebi's mini truck continues. At an afternoon stopover in La Ceiba, I watch Sebi's boyhood friends—now retired elders like him—sit under a shady tree playing a card game. I listen to Sebi and Matun praise Sebi's friend Junior, a former soccer player and the father of Joshua, who plays the sport for Honduras. It's a playful and nostalgic moment on a street corner, with stories of Sebi's grandmother Mama Hay circling the group, along with memories of my hometown, Washington, D.C., a flagship location for Sebi's budding herbal business.

"That was because of Adio Kuumba," he recalls in a conversation. Adio Akil Kuumba, a naturalist in her own right, met Sebi in Frederiksted, a west end town in St. Croix, Virgin Islands, where she studied natural healing and food therapy at the Garden Holistic Institute. She witnessed Sebi's success healing people in St. Croix and told him black communities in the United States longed for the sustainable alternative healing he provided. Since the Nation of Islam and the Mexican herbalist had already informed Sebi about diseases and food in black communities, it was an easy sell. Adio convinced him to set up shop in the States. She introduced Sebi to those communities around 1982—Washington, D.C., was one of the first.

"But I liked it because what I found out, you women, you D.C. women, are all industrious women. Oh yes, and there are so many of you guys. For every man there's about twelve women in D.C., right?"

"I think that's about it," I say, as we laugh together. One of his boyhood friends joins us.

"That's why I want to go to D.C.," he jokes.

"D.C. is beautiful, and the people are lovely. I love D.C. I love D.C., and D.C. gave me a bunch, a lot of love too." He segues to some business at hand. "So I got a phone number here from this lady whose father, grandfather used to give us a place to live. Many times my grandmother didn't have a place to stay, I mean any money to pay. But you see, now I grew up to do them a favor to compensate for what my grandmother didn't have. That's the way life is. So I got the number here."

"Life is beautiful," I say, as I watch and listen to him honor his grandmother's memory.

He agrees and repeats, "Life is always beautiful."

The fellas that grew up with Sebi are playing the game Casino underneath a tree when we stop by. A comedic side of Sebi rears its head when he introduces them.

"Yeah. This is my cousin. Chaptor younger than I am. That's the one over there. Bill is younger than I am too but he grew up with us, you could say. Well, Tom is old as shit."

"Not much older than you," Tom shoots back. Everybody laughs.

"And then there's Mostell, which is not here. He isn't here," he says softly. Dogs are barking behind house gates and the radio is on. "So this is the world."

"Sebi's world," I say.

"This is Sebi's world. The person that you all know in America as Dr. Sebi, well, he grew up under mango trees. He was eating boiled banana with coconut oil on it sometimes. But he was never poor." He chuckles.

Regardless of his financial situation, either as a little boy living underneath a house with his family or as a child and teenager working to pay living expenses for himself and Mama Hay, Sebi never claimed poverty. Just minutes earlier he recalled his grandmother's lack of money for housing, yet the words "poor" and "poverty" never crossed his lips. It's time to ask his friends about their relationship with Sebi and Mama Hay.

"What did you used to call him? We call him Dr. Sebi. What did you call him?" One of the guys says Fred, but Sebi wants a different answer.

"No, before Fred," he instructs.

Tom says Mama Hay.

"Mama Hay?"

"Mama Hay," he repeats.

"Why did you call him Mama Hay?"

"Well, because of his grandmother. I don't know whether it was her real name, but we called her Mama Hay. She's the one that reared him. So we called him, we just pinned him Mama Hay by his grandmother name."

"Did you know her?"

"Yes."

"What was she like?"

"She was very nice. As usual, most Hondurans are nice."

I ask if he and the others can talk about how Mama Hay influenced Sebi. Tom doesn't know. Sebi watches them play cards, then offers to buy peach juice for everybody. As the game goes on, I continue to gather stories about Mama Hay and Sebi.

"What's the real Fred or Mama Hay really like?"

"Miss Ann?" Bill asked.

"Yes."

"Miss Ann was a nice lady. Fred used to be more like her son. Made up of the aunt and all the Bowmans and mother."

"What was Fred like coming up?"

"Heard he was always moving fast."

"Moving fast? Where was he going, moving so fast?" I ask.

"His work," Bill answers. "In the commissary he used to work. Yeah, he used to work in the commissary. That's what I know mostly about Fred. That's all I could tell you because afterwards Fred went on a ship and it would be long before I saw Fred. It would be thirteen, fourteen years before I see him again."

"Okay, so Tom were you real close to Sebi?"

"No, I used to live here. They lived in the town."

"Was Mama Hay like Sebi, tall?"

"Yeah, almost as tall as him."

Wow. Sebi was six foot three. That's pretty tall for a woman. I was thinking they must be descendants of the Maasai tribe, the tallest men and women in Africa, with men capable of jumping more than two feet off the ground. The conversation continues outdoors with Sebi's friends, including a younger man with fewer memories of Sebi.

"I know him as Dr. Sebi."

"You don't know him as Fred? No," I self-correct, "because that was—"

"Bill would know that," Sebi jumps in. "Everybody go Mama Hay! Mama Hay! I got used to Mama Hay. You're Mama Hay, because it was me and Mama Hay. Anywhere Mama Hay went, I was there, holding on to her prop." He gives a short laugh.

"I hear she was just as tall as you were," I say.

"Yes, she was. Tall, with two big plaits, with a rope down on her side. Fuck around with my grandmother motherfuckers—"

"And what will happen?" I smile and ask.

"You get your ass kick." Hearty laughter fills the air. We find Sebi's remark quite funny. Matun too, but she steers the conversation to sports.

"Was it Junior son we saw on that soccer game?"

"One day we woke up," Sebi recounts, "we flicked the TV on, and who do we see in Miami? Your son driving the ball. Joshua, yeah."

Junior sits under the tree with us. He played professional soccer too.

"He left a record that's unbroken, right?" Sebi says. "No one ever broke his record."

"So now his son is playing," I say.

"He's the goalkeeper, though. Yeah, he's bad. He's tough," Sebi boasts.

"He plays for Honduras?"

"Yeah. I think he's going to play for the Selection, huh?" Sebi asks.

Obviously humbled by all the accolades for his son, Junior nods yes.

"You see? He's going to play for the Selection of Honduras. Junior was good," Sebi continues, beaming. He speaks as if he were watching Junior play and cheering him on that moment. I'm struck by his sixty-year-old friendship with Junior, Tom, and Bill. Even though they traveled different roads from boyhood to their seventies, they managed to return to the mango tree and relate. I wonder what more I'll discover in the days ahead.

Back at Usha, we relax in Sebi's home. He bathes and talks while Matun and I sit in the front area of his cabin, a 350-square-foot studio. The topic is childbirth and health in Honduras. Sebi knows it well. He's delivered babies at Usha and other homes.

"Are there hospitals here or no?" I ask.

"See, you don't go to hospitals to have babies," Sebi exclaims.

"That's where you go to bring disease. People with disease go to a hospital. A newborn baby doesn't have any disease. Why does she have the baby in the hospital?"

"Okay. That makes sense," I say. Thoughts of midwives (my late mother included), birthing centers, and doulas enter my mind.

"And she was born with her little girl, and the candles and the beautiful music, and the baby came. Like all babies just come. Saama was born over there."

"Really?" My initial response is a blend of surprise and awe. But I soon realize it makes perfect sense for Sebi to deliver his daughter in a natural environment like Usha.

"In that hut over there," he continues, "Saama was born over there."

"In the green one?"

"Yeah, the last one. It's common here for babies to be born at home. We breastfeed here. In America, it's a bottle with animal milk in it."

I agree, but only to a certain extent. If women in America feel uncomfortable breastfeeding, or newborns simply won't take mommy's breastmilk, baby formula is the go-to alternative—not the best alternative, but one some mothers in the United States rely on. "We love conveniences," I say, to which Matun replies, "What's more convenient than your breast?"

Black Women Encourage His Healing Journey

In the 1970s, Afrocentric black women in Los Angeles had as much to do with Sebi's metamorphosis as the Mexican who healed him and the grandmother who raised him. They helped him chart a course of objective listening and diligent herbalism that served him for more than forty years. The following section is an excerpt from the transcript of my 2005 interview with Sebi. It puts you front and center in our conversation about those engaging women. Sebi continues to bathe and speak, while Matun and I listen and rest after a day's tour of La Ceiba. Notice the shift from the biographical to a gradual crossing over from a state of dis-ease to ease.

SEBI: They told me Fumilayo went to Germany and she became a photographer.

BEVERLY: Right.

SEBI: You know her?

BEVERLY: No, I don't know Fumilayo, un-uh.

SEBI: Yeah. But those women were powerful, boy. Those women were bad.

BEVERLY: It was Linda and who else?

SEBI: Huh?

BEVERLY: It was Linda and who else?

SEBI: And Fumilayo and Aduwa.

BEVERLY: Aduwa? That name sounds familiar.

SEBI: They were bad. They were some badass women, boy.

BEVERLY: And they were all vegetarian?

SEBI: Yes, except Aduwa, and Aduwa died in 1994 in Chicago. That was a hell of a story boy.

BEVERLY: Why was that a hell of a story?

SEBI: Oh, that was one hell of a story.

BEVERLY: Her death?

SEBI: Remember when I talk about the thirty-four women having a party at my house and they were all naked?

BEVERLY: Yes, yes.

SEBI: Aduwa was one of those women. But Aduwa was the only one who was eating meat. All the other women are alive except her. She died in Chicago of breast cancer.

BEVERLY: Oh, yes, yes.

SEBI: You see? And she remembered when I told her that. She said, "Don't tell me I told you so." I said I'm aware. I don't have to, because that wouldn't be proper. That wouldn't be right.

BEVERLY: But did that also affect your healing, your healing too, your wanting to be healed?

SEBI: What you say?

BEVERLY: Did that also affect your healing, meeting Fumilayo and Linda?

SEBI: No, it didn't. They saw healing in me and I denied it.

BEVERLY: Oh, okay.

SEBI: They saw healing in me before I saw healing in me and I denied it. And they said, "Yes, you are a healer." They even took me to a woman at the uh, on Adams, that sells candles and all kinds of stuff. They took me there that afternoon around one or two o'clock. And I was pissed at these women. But the woman said,

"Why don't you do what you supposed to be doing?"

I said, "How in the hell you know so much about me more than I know about myself?"

And the woman said, "You know what you should be doing."

I said, "I don't know." And I didn't know. But ten years later I was a healer.

BEVERLY: That's great.

SEBI: Isn't that something girl?

BEVERLY: Yes.

SEBI: Yeah, yeah. You guys, but you guys compromise yourself to men. My mama didn't. My mama said she didn't believe a thing my father had to say. She liked him but she didn't have to trust his judgment.

BEVERLY: Right.

SEBI: She wasn't stupid.

BEVERLY: So when you left that party what did you do?

SEBI: I didn't leave the party. The party was in my house. All these naked women.

BEVERLY: Oh my.

SEBI: I enjoyed it because I didn't see it as an orgy, no. Naked women to me doesn't represent that, girl. No. A woman's body represents more than just sex.

BEVERLY: Right.

SEBI: Yeah.

BEVERLY: So it was an American woman that told you to go and do what you're supposed to do, right?

SEBI: It was a black woman from America on Adams, yes. Linda, Fumilayo, and another one named Maquenta took me there, took me to that woman, and when I got there, the woman said, "Why don't you do what you're supposed to be doing?"

BEVERLY: Was she a psychic?

SEBI: She used to sell candles.

BEVERLY: She sold candles. Right. But she wasn't psychic.

SEBI: I don't know what that is.

BEVERLY: Well, I mean, people like Mama Hay said,

SEBI: Make them smile.

BEVERLY: Yeah, okay, like Mama Hay could look at cards and see things. You know, this woman told you, asked you why aren't you doing what you're supposed to do.

SEBI: But that is being psychic?

BEVERLY: Oh, I don't know.

SEBI: Okay, that's what I'm saying. Those words fucked with me.

BEVERLY: I know. I know.

SEBI: Because see, Mama Hay, I could see it now. And I didn't go to school to learn anything about neuropathology or psychology. You could look at a person and tell that they are stressed, and all you have to do is this. (Sebi pulls up a chair in front of me and looks in my eyes.) "Tell me the truth. What's bothering you?" Boy, right there they swear that you done read the inside of them. But that happens to everybody. Then they begin to open their mouth. And as they open their mouth, the psychic begins to extrapolate from all of that, and then she play it back. And the person didn't know that she told the psychic the whole story. That's the way it is.

BEVERLY: Right. Right.

SEBI: You listen, Beverly. You listen. How did I do my first consultation? I wasn't trained. I let the patient talk.

BEVERLY: Right, and so you just recommended things for the patient to take?

SEBI: No. I already knew what to recommend because I make one treatment. I don't make treatment special for AIDS or diabetes. It's the same treatment.

BEVERLY: It's just one thing.

SEBI: It's one thing. It's one disease. So, I didn't have to go through psychoanalyzing anyone. No. That's pseudoscience. No. People came here that were schizophrenic. People came here with delirium tremors. People came here that were paranoid. And people came here with Parkinson's, and they all left cured. Well, how did that happen? How did it happen? The African Bio Mineral Electric Cell food. Okay? Now, you talk about the yin yang. That's Chinese. You talk about the macrobiotic. That's Japanese. And you talk about the ayurvedic. That's Indian. You talk about allopathic or homeopathic. That's European. But nowhere did I hear my momma. So you mean to tell me that no black man in America, or Honduras, Africa or anywhere couldn't come up with something that represent Momma? Come on, now. The Chinese did. The Japanese did.

The Indian did. How come we didn't? That's why this is not Sebism. This is a black woman that has been forgotten! And she herself has fallen victim to the same thing the European woman fell victim to. You all following men. So, you should kick your ass because you follow him. He should mislead you because you're following him.

BEVERLY: I'm following, I want to follow you, but you're following women?

SEBI: [*chuckles*]

BEVERLY: I'm following you, but of course when I follow you, I'm following Mama Hay.

SEBI: You're not following me Beverly. You know what you're following?

BEVERLY: What am I following?

SEBI: You're following not Sebi because Sebi is not following Sebi either.

BEVERLY: Oh, you're following Mama Hay.

SEBI: No!

BEVERLY: You're following the cosmic arrangement.

SEBI: Ah-ha!

BEVERLY: Cosmic arrangement of life.

SEBI: That principle, girl.

BEVERLY: That principle—cosmic arrangement of life.

SEBI: That's right. Sebi doesn't know a thing.

BEVERLY: Divine order.

SEBI: Thank you! That's all Sebi's doing. Sebi is not a wise man. Sebi is not an intelligent man. Sebi is not a stupid man. Sebi is none of that. Sebi is Sebi. Makes it easy now. Makes it easy. You are just as cosmic as I am because you were made by the same energy. How can I be more cosmic than you? I may understand it a little bit more. That's all. And when you understand it, you will see that you will know more than I know because you are a woman. You're a female. But that's where my wife come in. [*points to Matun*] That's why this woman knows that there can be no man on this planet as smart as her, because she knows that all men came out of the vagina of a woman. And she's the one that put it into his head, inculcated into his head the primary basic understanding of life come from momma and not from a school.

"In my book I said that the only black man on the planet that I respect is the black man of America, because it is the truth. What he has done, nobody else has. Name another one. Yes, I've had the negative thrown to me by some of them because they were negative. But I've had beautiful things thrown to me because they were beautiful. Just like the old man in the village. The old man is living on the edges of the village. And the traveler came to the village and asked the old man,

'Old Man! What kind of people live here?'

'Why?'

'The village I just left, they are cutthroats!'

The old man said, 'The same kind of people live here.'

So he turned back. Another traveler next month came.

'Old man, what kind of people live here?'

The old man said, 'Why?'

'Because the village I just left? They beautiful. They nice.'

He said, 'The same kind of people live here.'

"So in America you would find a percentage of brothers who carry pain, and they gonna exhibit that pain by trying to offend others, but they're only offending themselves. But in America you'll find black people, who, like you describe so many times to me, that I have been with them and interrelated from Beaufort to Charleston to Winston-Salem. I've been around the United States. And I have met black people that live the way I would like to live. Well, I met some that's just the opposite. So what is the percentage? I don't know. I hope that the people that complement are the majority. But, like I said, the only people in America that's black and have rejected this outwardly are the leaders. Nobody else, because the common people come to me like myself, because I'm common. I'm not the family of the Rosenberg, or I'm not the family of the Johnsons. No. I didn't start this business with a springboard of a million dollars. I started this with $300. Without any education. So I know that I am the common folk."

Los Angeles and the Letter to Elijah Muhammad

By 2005, at age seventy-two, Sebi had settled down in Honduras after more than fifty years of world travel, fifty years of observing and immersing himself in multicultural experiences, including those in Los Angeles. We're in his cabin at Usha one evening. In his mind's eye he journeys back to a time in L.A., when he's separated from Melba, his first wife, and living a single life. Speaking as if he's still living in those days, he recalls friendships, neighbors, and his own actions, and the impression each one left on him.

"Oh God, I used to do things that I want to know how, where did I get that energy from because it frightens me."

"Was it the music?" I ask. I know he loves jazz.

"No, I used to be doing all kinds of stuff, girl. I used to drive to Lake Arrowhead, come back in the same night, or go south and see, stay there for days in the desert. I did a whole lot of beautiful things with me."

"Did you listen to the music driving along?"

"Oh yes, always."

"What is it Weather Report? I've heard of them. I don't know their music."

"Their music is beautiful. I like it. There's one playing, known as *Mysterious Traveler*. But let me say this. I don't know if this woman is in the book. But this woman is a woman that was living next to me. And, I don't know if she is going to read this book. But this was the only person in my life that did this to me. I was living at 12524 Birch."

"In L.A.?"

"In L.A., and next door to me was this girl named—it's a French name. I'll remember her name in a minute."

"Renée?"

"No. I'll remember it. I was staying there for approximately two years I think, or three, maybe longer. And she came to me on my birthday. Nicole came to my door, and I wondered how did she do that. I say,

'How you know today was my birthday?'

She said, 'Look, those walls are very thin, and you have a very resonating voice. I know every sex act. I know every woman name. I know everything more than you realize I know about you. But today is your birthday, and I bring you this.'

And she gave me a book. I say, 'I don't read books.'

She say, 'You gonna read this book because this is the book of your life.'

"The book was titled *The Morning of the Magicians*. She did that. Another one that lived in the same complex saw me baking bread at two o'clock in the morning. It was a Saturday, so she wanted to know why would I be home baking bread. Well, what you want me to do? I'm baking this good bread that I'm going to eat. I learned to bake bread because my grandmother taught me how to bake bread and also my mother. So at two o'clock Saturday morning I'm baking bread because I don't have anything to do. I was listening to music. I was high anyway. And I was feeling good. And

I started to bake bread. So she was coming from the streets and she asked me,

'You mean to tell me you cannot find something better to do than to bake bread?'

I said, 'Well, I think that the bread I'm baking is gonna have the taste that I want it to have, and I'm gonna enjoy this bread. Yeah.'

"But I was doing a lot of things. I was experimenting. I was, oh, I was happy. I was happy. I remember that. I was happy. I was happy like I am now but it was a different expression of happiness. I knew this brother by the name of Chaka. I knew Lee Drawn. I like Lee Drawn. Of all the people that I met in my life, as a brother, Lee Drawn was the smoothest, the cleanest, the most considerate. I like him. I like him. I never saw Lee Drawn get into an argument with anyone. Lee Drawn always had a beautiful laughing way to soothe it over. But something happened between Lee Drawn and I. I love this man so very much and I respect him, and he flies planes too. Lee Drawn invited me to come to his house. And I promised I was coming because he had come to my house and ate what I cooked, and he liked it. So he wanted to show me that he could do the same thing. And I was going to Lee Drawn that Sunday. He lived in Camarillo. And guess what? That Sunday was when me and Marilyn were going through the separation. It was a big thing. And Lee Drawn never knew that. And I don't know if he's comfortable with that because I was uncomfortable, and I didn't go to Lee Drawn house. I love Lee Drawn. Yes. And there was a minister, his name, he's from Pasadena. Uh, what is his name? But he was Lee Drawn's friend. And he was beautiful too. So I met some very beautiful brothers in L.A. Lee Drawn was from Philadelphia. Yeah. He flies planes. He's a teacher, yeah. And I know he's a good teacher because he, Lee Drawn, could explain things well. He was very intricate. He was very precise, focused. Oh yeah, Lee Drawn. I miss him."

"You had some good times in L.A.," I say, watching the beam in his eyes.

"Yeah, I have some good times with everybody. Everybody like me and I like everybody. And I'm saying that including Ron Karenga. Ron doesn't hate me, and how can I hate Ron when Ron is one of us, right?"

Ron Karenga, now known as Dr. Maulana Karenga, is the creator of the African American and Pan-African holiday Kwanzaa.

Sebi continues. "But there was always a little thing between me and Ron because I could never digest what Ron was delivering. And it could have been because I came from such a culture that just couldn't process certain things. And this is why I couldn't get into debates about the dialectics, Karl Marx, and socialism. I could not understand those things because I come from an environment where corn and beans is the thing of the day. Corn and beans, and then we jump in a little boat and go get a fish. And we were satisfied. Now I have to be deciphering what Karl Marx said and also Socrates. Now how can I do that?" Sebi asks and chuckles. "I couldn't devote any energy to that, you know. But Lee didn't talk that way though. Lee was pragmatic. Yeah, he was. I remember Lee Drawn, oh yes, in so many beautiful ways. I wish I could see him again. I wish I could see him again."

"Does he still live in California?"

"Yeah, he lives in L.A. And I saw him. I looked for him recently, and I think I found him. Where I went and found him? I think it was Pasadena. Anybody would love Lee Drawn. Any woman would love Lee Drawn. Oh, he's graceful. Oh, he's bad. He's a bad brother. He's bad. Look, I can't say enough. But then there was another brother there that I loved equally, and he helped me tremendously, Gregory MacLemore. He worked with me. MacLemore, yeah. The great MacLemore. That's right. His wife told me that they been married for seventeen years and he talk about me every day." Sebi chuckles. "But what she doesn't know is that I talk about him every day. You see, my relationship with people, whether male or female, I'm not going to have a relationship with you unless that relationship is based on love and affection, because I'm not going to be your friend if I'm uncomfortable with you. I'm not going to be around you because I become uncomfortable. I'm going to put space, because it may be my own, my own immaturity why I have felt a way, or maybe you have done something to me. That's the only time that I know that I put space between me and you. It's that you have done something.

"Like when I was sent to Chicago with a very incriminating letter to Elijah Muhammad condemning Malcolm, and the brother that sent that, well, I don't think that I really wanted to be around him anymore because I didn't want to be part of conspiracy. Why do I have to be part of conspiracy? I mean, I already know that life is about food, clothing, and shelter. Where does the conspiracy come in? I don't know. But if we devote our time towards doing these things for ourselves and the African people, well, that's another thing there. That's another story there, for the African people."

And so the rejection begins, in Africa, no less. To speak of dembali is to speak of history because, according to Sebi, rejection and conditioning are born in the past. He sets aside his mellow accolades for Lee Drawn and his memories of other friends in Los Angeles. The storm in his voice signals rocky waters ahead. Certain topics affect Sebi that way—politicians and doctors, and, ironically, African politicians and doctors top the list. Needless to say, these groups, in the past, rejected his herbal medicine. But it was the ultimate betrayal when the health experts in Africa shunned Sebi's methods, even though it was his mission in life to help people of African heritage with the health issues they encountered adapting to modern Western culture.

"The African people are aware that when they took us away from Africa, we didn't have any passport. But now that we want to go back to Africa, you better have a passport! You understand me?"

"Thank you for mine by the way. Thank you for the passport," I say.

"Thank you for the passport?" he echoes, with a puzzled look that says 'What does that have to do with anything?'

"Yes, my passport."

"What happened?"

I didn't have one at the time. I never had one. I remember a time when there were lenient and convenient travel rules and procedures. Any legal ID sufficed at airports, so I used my driver's license when I traveled to Canada and the three times I vacationed in the Caribbean islands. I hadn't considered a passport until Sebi mentioned I'd need one to get to Honduras. I greatly appreciated his generosity.

"Thank you," I repeat.

"No, but I'm saying," he continues, unfazed by his act of kindness. "I'm saying when we left, when they took us away from Africa, we didn't have a passport. But for us to go back to Africa, we need a passport. They took us away without a passport. Why do we need one to go back now? Is that an African rule? Is that an African way of life? Is that the African way of life we left when they took us away? That now I can't go back home because I don't have a passport? That's the Africa of today. Regardless to the color of your skin and your heritage. It means absolutely nothing. You don't have a passport. Hey, my brother African, did you invent this passport? Did you draw these borders? No. Well, why do you want to apply this to me? Because he has to. He has to, regardless of the ancestors."

Dis-Ease

HIV/AIDS and African Americans
Source: U.S. Office of Minority Health

- Although African Americans represent 13% of the U.S. population, they account for 44% of HIV infection cases in 2016.
- In 2016, African Americans were 8.4 times more likely to be diagnosed with HIV infection, as compared to the white population.

Ease

Chapter: Agua Caliente—Usha Village
Source: Dr. Sebi, *Seven Days in Usha Village: A Conversation with Dr. Sebi*

I trusted my judgment. Why? Because I selected plants whose molecular structure is complete, which deems them electrical; and so is the human body. But when the individual that had AIDS was cured, Mr. White, then I was encouraged to know or when the blind man was seeing, I was further encouraged.

Section 2—His Work

Natural Healing on Trial

Regardless of the number of people Sebi and the Fig Tree healed, someone, somewhere tipped off authorities in New York City government that Sebi was just a man giving out herbs to the public, not a bona fide doctor. In July 1987 Alfredo Bowman had his day in court, with Judge Kenneth L. Shorter presiding. Other parties in the trial included petitioners Robert Abrams, the attorney general of the State of New York; Phyllis Spaeth, assistant attorney general of the State of New York; and respondents Ogun Herbal Research Institute, doing business as Usha Herbal Research Institute; Maa Bowman and Fig Tree Products.

PRESENT:
HON. KENNETH L. SHORTER, Justice
————————————————————X
PEOPLE OF THE STATE OF NEW YORK, by :
ROBERT ABRAMS, Attorney General of
The State of New York, :
Petitioners, :
– against– :
OGUN HERBAL RESEARCH INSTITUTE :
d/b/a USHA HERBAL RESEARCH INSTITUTE;
ALFRED0 BOWMAN a/k/a DR. SEBI; :
MAA BOWMAN and FIG TREE PRODUCTS
COMPANY, :
Respondents. :
————————————————————X

Text from the Judgment and Order on Consent page

The television is on, the volume low. Low-wattage light from a small lamp on the nightstand is bright enough for the right side of Sebi's king-sized bed, leaving the opposite side of the cabin where I sit dim. I ease my body into the soft cushion of the futon sofa across from Sebi's bed as the recorder continues to roll. I ask him about an experience that still leaves an aftertaste in his mouth—his arrest in New York.

"There's this whole New York thing that I would like to get into, like the day they came and your photographer friend—"

"Oh, Martin Baugh."

"Martin Baugh, your photographer friend. Yeah, that was an interesting day I'll bet."

"He looked out the window and say, 'Hey man, your day has arrived.'

I say, 'Yeah?'

'There's Channel 13, there's Channel 2, there's Channel 7 outside your window.'

And five seconds later they were kicking the door down."

"Wow," is all I can say.

"Understand? Whatever they were going to do warrant that, kicking the door down. 'Get this nigga out of here. What do you mean he's curing AIDS? Crazy!'"

"Well, why did they come with such force? Why did they do that?" I could understand it if they were raiding a crack house, but a healer?

"Why? Why shouldn't they do that? They represent the police. That's why when Channel 7 asked me, 'Dr. Sebi, do you really cure AIDS?' I said, my response was, I cure AIDS then. I cure AIDS now. And for as long as I live I will be able to cure AIDS. Then the next question from them was, 'Well, how do you feel to be arrested?' I said the police have to do things the police way."

FROM THE RAINFOREST TO THE USA

The police handcuffed Sebi on February 10, 1987 and took him to jail, where he shared a cell with a crack dealer, an embezzler, and a murderer. He had conversations with all of them, including a whopper of a story from the crack dealer, an alleged crack dealer Sebi soon discovered. The West Indian man told him about his arrest. As it turned out, the man sold pieces of frozen cocaine-resembling Palmolive soap that failed to measure up to the real thing. Gone was the euphoric high his customers craved. The fake dope discouraged many of his customers so much that they stopped using crack, which Sebi considered pure genius on the West Indian's part. The herbalist and the crack dealer, on a mission to take people from a state of dis-ease to ease.

After representing himself in court and having more than seventy witnesses testify on his behalf, Sebi won his case. In 1988 his eight-year-old son, Sesa, watched as the jury returned a verdict of not guilty on all charges: practicing medicine without a license, selling products not approved by the American Medical Association, falsely claiming to cure AIDS and other diseases. And not only that, the presiding New York Supreme Court judge on the case, Anne Feldman, became one of Sebi's clients. Judge Feldman died April 27, 2016, at the age of eighty-six.

By the time Sebi and I see each other again in 2005, his cure for AIDS and the controversy it caused in New York City is legendary and part of his autobiography, *The Cure*. Sebi freely gives the details again but he's defensive when he recalls what happened to him in New York City's Consumer Affairs Office and on the phone with Assistant Attorney General Phyllis Spaeth. The story is brand new to me so I listen carefully to make sure it's fully covered in Sebi's edited autobiography.

"I intend to write a book," he says, "based on what brought healing to the forefront. Never in my thoughts was there a name that would be placed in there that was cured of any of the diseases. No. So now, in putting people's names in the book would be compromising my integrity. This book is written to show the world that what is going to happen is going to happen regardless, but this is the outcome of that particular journey. And they will put in the book the diagnostic sheets about AIDS. Meaning that will be the only thing in the book to show the world, yes, we cure AIDS. Well, if we could cure AIDS, what disease is there that is as devastating as AIDS? None."

"A lady had a brother that was in Boston in the hospital with AIDS, and you cured him of that. Around this time you started to run an ad in the *Amsterdam News* and the *Park Slope* paper about healing AIDS, right?" I ask.

"That AIDS has been cured by the Usha Research Institute and we specialize in cures for sickle cell, lupus, herpes, cancer, blindness, impotence and others."

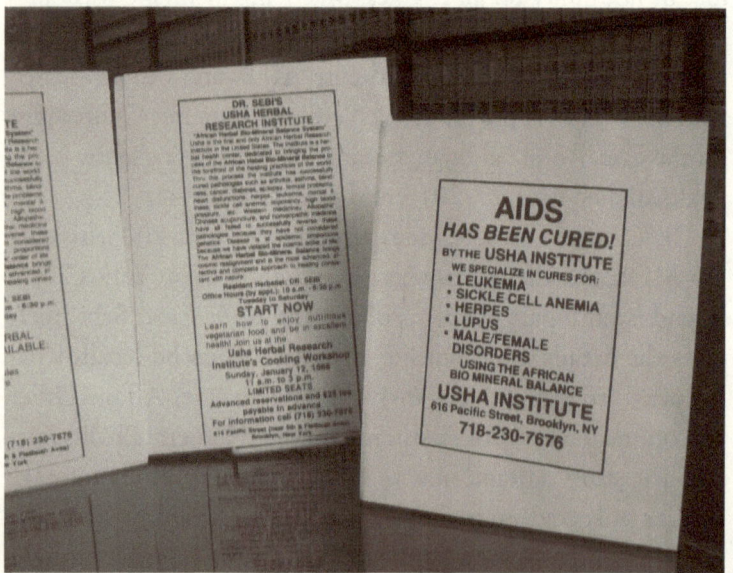

Sebi's advertisements

"Okay, great. So right around this time you started seeing some strange things happening, like white people started coming around asking questions, right?"

"Yes."

"Was this around 1985, 1986?" I ask.

"1986. They were coming around asking those crazy questions. And because I was, according to them, arrogant, they couldn't understand a black man standing up in defense of himself, because they never had that presented to them before, so they thought this had to be destroyed."

"The guy that came around, what crazy questions was he asking you?"

"Same kind of questions everybody ask, trying to incriminate you. I can't go into the specifics but they were incriminating questions, you know, questions to incriminate me then. But I didn't care, because I gave him exactly what I wanted him to have, and exactly what I wanted him to hear, and exactly what he came to hear. But yet he couldn't use it. You see, people live in fear. I don't fear God or the devil because I don't live in fear. And many people live in fear. So, because they use themselves as a yardstick, they imagine that nobody else in the world live outside of fear. Well, I don't give a damn about anything. So, being that way, the Puerto Rican didn't know that I already knew that the question he was asking, without asking for medicine, he had to be a cop. But it didn't matter, because what was I doing that was so illegit? Nothing. So why should I be afraid if he was a cop?"

Afterward, Sebi received a telegram from Assistant Attorney General Spaeth.

"And she said to please come to her office and bring with me all complaints that I may have received. And then her number was under the statement. So I called the number. I say, 'Miss

Phyllis Spaeth, you are requesting for me to appear at your office at such and such a date. But that is the date that I selected to be with my wife and my babies in Puerto Rico at Luquillo Beach.' She say, 'Do you know the power of the law?' I said, 'You better know it.' I slammed the phone down. You don't talk to me like that. Who you think I am?"

"So you were going on vacation at Luquillo Beach."

"I had promised my wife and my babies that I would be with them at Luquillo Beach on the day she wanted me to come to her office."

"Then she became indignant."

"Well I—so what?" He chuckles. "When I came back, then I had the summons to go to the Consumer Affairs Office this time. Well, I went to the Consumer Affairs Office, Mr. Fitzgerald, and he said,

'Are you responsible for this ad?'

I said yes.

And he said, 'That AIDS has been cured?'

I said yes.

'Well, I want you to remove the ad.'

I said, 'Sure. Why?'

He said, 'Many people have made claims and have yet to live up to their claims.'

I said, 'That's true. I know that to be a fact because I was a recipient of snake oil.[2] I went to UCLA Medical Center. I went to the Touro Infirmary. I went to the Memorial Hospital in Boston, and they didn't cure anything. So what you just said is true, because I got snake oil from them.'

He said, 'I don't understand.'

I said, 'I know that you don't understand.'

Then he said, 'Well, you're going to remove the ad anyway.'

I said, 'Oh yes? We have a little problem with that because the only person in the universe that will tell me to do something and I will carry that mandate out isn't the Virgin Mary or Jesus Christ. It happen to be my mother, and you happen not to be my mother. So how are we going to do this?'

"I walked out of his office. I didn't give a damn. What do you mean, because you say so? The only person that have the honor to get me to do something is my momma, not the Virgin Mary, especially Fitzgerald. You know where he is on the list. But to many people that shouldn't have been. But he had the right to offend me because he said so. Fitzgerald doesn't know the food that is consistent with our cellular predisposition. I know that Fitzgerald and nobody else in America knows that. I already know that. So after I walk out of his office, a month later he called me and said,

'You haven't removed the ad.'

I said, 'I have a sinking feeling that you're going to give me a reason why.'

He said, 'I'll see you in hell.'

That is what I received from the higher office in the government. That's the language."

Dis-Ease

Danai Gurira explains why World AIDS Day hits close to home
Source: Andrea Park, CBS News, November 2018

"Black Panther" and "Walking Dead" star Danai Gurira says World AIDS Day resonates with her because she saw the effects of the deadly disease in her own community when she was growing up. Gurira was born in the U.S. but grew up in Zimbabwe. "I witnessed its effect on society and communities and families."

Ease

Chapter: United States—New Beginnings
Source: Dr. Sebi, *Seven Days in Usha Village: A Conversation with Dr. Sebi*

So naturally, as I look at this arrangement of life, I find myself being very extremely careful, careful because I have not ever or do I remember wanting to be anything in my life. I want to be me. In the me, in the wanting to be me, I find that a whole lot of things came out of that, such as the healer. I'm not even convinced that the people who were cured of AIDS have been cured because there was not effort for me doing that. I could see myself doing it. I wonder why others are not doing so. Instead of them sharing with me, which is their responsibility to the world, not to me, because if I afford myself to the world as a healer, and I am not as responsive or I am not affording what others are affording, then it is my duty to visit those that are doing things on a higher level than I to learn how to help in complementing people in need.

Healing's Duality:
Rejection and Acceptance

A wide black sky speckled with glistening stars as far as the eye can see hovers over Usha, which means "healing." The property and the Usha Herbal Research Institute were named for Sebi and Maa's daughter.

It's evening in the rainforest, when nocturnal species fill the air with resonant croaks and chirps. Sebi lounges in his bed, his back and shoulders leaning on pillows pressed against the headboard. We continue talks about AIDS and the opposition he experienced despite having proof of his cures.

"Meharry Medical School couldn't have complimented me, even though I cured many people of diabetes that they know of. They cannot do it. I want the world to know that I knew before things happened. I knew what they were going to do, not only Meharry Medical School. I could name many other institutes, black institutes in America. They cannot do it."

"So Richard Pryor's wife saying no to you is just in line with Barbara King and"

"Everybody else," he finishes. Sebi offered his services to Richard Pryor when the late comedian suffered with multiple sclerosis.

"Maybe they want to see firsthand, Sebi, what you can do or what you've done. They don't want to go by hearsay. Maybe they need to see firsthand."

"I don't think that that would be used as a good excuse, because they have never seen the white man cure any disease and yet they continue to go there."

"That's their thinking Sebi," I say, unaware I'm treading on sensitive territory. The building is about to implode.

"Well, that's a poor excuse," he replies.

"Poor excuse. They're justified in what they do?"

"Yeah, poor, poor. That's poor," he repeats with greater volume.

"So you don't think they need to see evidence, they need to see proof?"

"Well, I got proof!" he shouts. "I got diagnostic sheets. That doesn't mean anything. What does it mean? I have the proof. So what? It's like Jack Johnson's black woman that told him in Galveston, 'For you to be with me you gotta fight a bull.' He fought the bull and win and she said, 'So.' So what. 'Sebi cures AIDS. So.' And Sebi knows that. Sebi knows that black America has been handicapped to the extent that it is extremely difficult for them to please their own self, to compliment themselves. And I represent them. I'm black."

I segue to talks of favorable experiences in Brooklyn, where neighborhood police embraced his work. Vanessa, a young African American bilingual English tutor with a background in anthropology is visiting Sebi, Matun, and me this evening. She looks as if she could be twenty-six or twenty-seven years old. She's from Brooklyn so she knows the city's vibe firsthand.

"I love Brooklyn, girl," Sebi tells her. We laugh and agree with him about Brooklyn's effect on people. "I love Brooklyn. Brooklyn is nice, and I love Brooklyn, and they love me there, even the police. The police in Brooklyn was on my side. One day, I was going to the store to buy something and a police say,

'Hey Dr. Sebi, are you going to buy that, are you going to eat that?'

I said, 'How do you know I'm Dr. Sebi?'

'Well, we know you. We call you Lightning.'

That was my nickname with the police, and then they started coming to see me. Like in L.A., we have a house full of police."

Dr. Sebi's client diagnosed with HIV

"Really?"

"All the time."

Of all the places that received Sebi well in his early days as a natural healer, Washington, D.C., my hometown, was one of them. D.C. provided a major hub for Sebi's teachings and healing. Wherever he spoke, the hall was packed to capacity (at least the lectures I attended in New York City and D.C.). In

> **HOSPITAL VICENTE D'ANTONI**
> DEPARTAMENTO DE LABORATORIO Y BANCO DE SANGRE
>
> Nombre: Zavala
>
> H.I.V = Negativo
>
> FECHA 13/enero/94

The same client diagnosed HIV negative after receiving treatment with Dr. Sebi's African Bio Mineral Balance Compounds

New York, saxophonist Hamiet Bluiett and conga player Tom "Taiwo" Duval often played background music for Sebi.

"What I saw was a bunch of beautiful black people and I still see that," Sebi recalls.

"What was the response like at the meetings at the Community Warehouse?"

"It was favorable. It was good. We always had a packed house."

The Community Warehouse sold bulk natural food and spices in northeast D.C., and provided meeting and event space. Sebi spoke there often and consulted clients in an upstairs office the Warehouse founders set up for him.

"It became very nice, very nice. I liked it. I like D.C. That's when I met Bernie McCain and he used to interview me on WHMM" (Howard University's public television station, now called WHUT). In addition to WHUT, other media wanted him.

"Well, Jimmy Stroud was one, because Jimmy Stroud heard about me," Sebi says. "And unlike the people from St. Croix that didn't believe me, black America, without even seeing me do the things I said I could do, they believed in me. So Jimmy Stroud was one."

When Sebi appeared at events in town, public radio broadcaster Jimmy Stroud announced it on his show at Pacifica radio station WPFW-FM. "He interviewed people, and he used to always send people to me, and he didn't even know me. And after all this time, two years, Jimmy Stroud appeared."

After eyewitnesses shared stories with him about Sebi's success as a healer, Jimmy sought Sebi's help for a member of his own family. His two-year-old daughter, Akila, suffered with sickle cell anemia, an oxygen-depleting disease common in black people. She received treatment for it at a Washington, D.C., hospital but Jimmy grew dissatisfied with Akila's slow, minimal progress. He removed her from the hospital's pediatric ward and followed the advice he gave to so many others. He turned to Dr. Sebi—the right decision, though bittersweet. Soon after Dr. Sebi healed Akila, the hospital ordered Jimmy to bring her back. The D.C. police assisted. Sebi recounts the story.

"The doctors felt that the little girl had not been properly treated. They summoned the mother, the father, and the little girl, and they went back with the little girl and me. And that was when they confronted me about, 'What kind of doctor are you?' I said, 'Yeah, how many kinds are there?' Then I asked them, because I realized they didn't know what is sickle cell. And then she told me that sickle cell was a situation that was presented to black people ten thousand years ago because their blood went to mutation. I said, 'But I'm confused because Dick Gregory said God gave us sickle cell to fight malaria. This is what Dick Gregory said at Cramton Auditorium at Howard University. Now lady, you are telling me that it wasn't God that gave us sickle cell. It was mutation. But lady, it's neither God nor mutation. It is the deprivation of iron fluorine."[3]

Jimmy Stroud made the ultimate decision for his daughter. He upheld Dr. Sebi's treatment and watched Akila survive. She reached a healthy twenty-year-old's life in 2004. Around the same time Sebi cured her, his eyes caught a notice on a bulletin board at Howard University Hospital. The Sickle Cell Anemia Research Foundation on Georgia Avenue in northwest D.C. had planned a meeting to address the disease.

"I was leaving the hospital from another situation. It was an African woman that had a baby, and she was suffering excruciating headaches. The doctors couldn't bring the headaches down. They couldn't stop the headache. Well, I knew what was wrong. A piece of the placenta was in the woman's uterus. But they didn't go to school to learn those things. My mother teach me that as a little boy. And I came with a little bottle, and the doctor told me that the only way that this bottle would be given to that lady is over his dead body. Well, the husband of the woman said, 'Give me the bottle.' And he stepped right over the doctor and went in to give it to his wife, and the headache left."

Sebi points to Matun. "On the way out is when she saw the bulletin board Sickle Cell Meeting on Georgia Avenue at the Sickle Cell Research Foundation. And she said, 'You have to go there.'"

Sebi went. He sat patiently through a hematologist's lecture about West African sickle cell anemia patients and the presence of lactatemia in their blood. The doctor attributed lactatemia to stress, a claim that caused Sebi to rise up from his seat and offer his insights. He told the hematologist that lactatemia is a derivative of lactic acid and that it had nothing to do with stress. Lactic acid comes from cow's milk. He told the doctor if he were really a responsible provider of health to the West African people, in reference to sickle cell anemia, he would never allow his patients to consume cow's milk, because cow's milk breaks down the mucus membrane.[4]

No matter how true his statements, another doctor at the meeting commanded Sebi to shut up and sit down. *The gall of an uninvited person to say such things to such a credentialed hematologist. Sit down and shut up man with no degree, man with no bona fide organization to vouch for you.* This is the sentiment that medically-, scientifically-, and politically-trained people harbored for Sebi, the man who had just cured Akila Stroud of sickle cell anemia.

Despite his achievements, it seems even Dr. Sebi, the autodidactic healer, needs a dose of dembali. I'm caught off guard when he condemns his business, telling me he wasted his time in America. How can this be when I, like countless others, represent proof of his success? Sebi hurls statistics at me that weaken the proof. Then, as if they were standing right in front of him in his cabin, he scolds opposers who want evidence that he cured AIDS and other diseases. It's a contentious moment.

"But you can't tell that to Americans, because America doesn't know what is natural. So you're going to spend your time wasting your time, because I've wasted thirty-one years in America," he gripes.

I can't believe what I'm hearing. The debate starts, teacher and disciple at loggerheads. "No you haven't," I chide. "No, you haven't wasted your time. Don't say that Sebi. You have not wasted your time. You have made a difference."

"In how many people's lives? I didn't even make a difference in my own mother's life or my own family life, talk about America."

"You've made a difference in my life. Doesn't that count for something?"

"Hold it. That doesn't account to anything in forty million people. That's not even a drop in the bucket."

"But that's a difference. You made a difference," I argue.

"But it's not. It's not," he says, steadfast.

I refuse to let him kick his work to the curb, even in the face of his baobab-strong rebuttals. I've kept asthma at bay because of his teaching that my beloved mac and cheese lays out the welcome mat for mucus that clogs my lungs and air passages. How can I not speak up for that?

"It's an example of what could be done," I insist.

"You know, hold it. Hold it. It would make a difference if 51 percent had accepted it and 49 didn't. Then! I said. But we touched about thirty thousand people out of forty million. It doesn't even show. So we know what the deal is. But in Latin America, we don't have to sell ourself the way we have to sell ourself in America."

"Alcida's father, who is he?" Matun asks. She knows what I'm driving at. She knows I'm right because she reminds Sebi of one of his achievements, an extraordinary one.

"Who?" he asks.

"Alcida, who was in, the little girl who was in a coma."

"That had leukemia," he recalls.

"Yeah."

"What happened?" Sebi asks, trying to identify his client.

"Who was in the coma. Who was she?"

He remembers. "She was the little girl that had leukemia that the mayor brought to me." He doesn't mention the mayor's name or city.

"The mayor. The mayor's daughter," Matun says proudly.

Others vouch for Sebi—today and before he died. His herbal medicine struck a chord with author and certified plant-based nutritionist Aqiyl Aniys. He wrote *Alkaline Herbal Medicine: Reverse Disease and Heal the Electric Body*, a book that helps explain why Sebi used alkaline herbs in his African Bio Mineral Balance system.

> The alkaline movement is running strong, thanks to the work of the herbalist Dr. Sebi, who has spearheaded the alkaline movement with his African Bio Mineral Balance… Many herbalists use various herbs to reverse disease. Dr. Sebi has been instrumental in identifying the natural alkaline herbs…herbs whose chemical composition hasn't been compromised through hybridization and genetic modification.

When there is no enemy within, the enemies outside can't hurt you.
It's not what you are called, but what you answer to.

—African proverbs

"Well, it is true," Sebi says. "Why should I hide what happened, what occurred?"

He's retired now, with plenty of time to reflect on the peaks and valleys of his life.

"One brother said I was lying. The white man said I was ignorant, and the other brother said I was a nappy-head nigga. And I said you're right to all of them. I have no problem giving people right. Remember, I grew up in a time, in an environment where it is said, and continue to practice, that the respect of other people's right is peace. I didn't lose anything by giving them right. They right. You see, it's easy with me. 'Dr. Sebi, you're a liar.' You're right. 'Dr. Sebi, my grandmother love you.' Thank you. You see, it doesn't matter."

"It's all the same," I say.

"It's all the same because I'm already in my element. I've been in my element since I met this woman (Matun) twenty years ago, twenty-five years ago. I'm happy."

"What would you prefer to do? At this point in your life you prefer—to just chill, not really take on the mechanics of running a business?"

"Well, I'm not a businessman. I know nothing about business. I came to heal people, but people equate business and healing together, when I am not a businessman. I own a business, but I am not a businessman."

"So who put the beautiful labels that you have on the bottles, whose idea was that? The labels, when I saw that I said, 'Wow, look at Sebi's new labels!' when I came to Los Angeles. I was used to the white bottles. So who put all that together? Whose idea was that?"

"I don't know."

"Oh Sebi." A limp and aloof stranger sits before me. What's going on? Come on, Sebi.

"I don't know. I really don't know. Maybe her, maybe the girls."

"Who's the one that put the sayings on the bottles, and the address and Lancaster, Pennsylvania? Who designed all that?" I continue.

"That was designed by, what, China?" he asks Matun, referring to his assistant China Robinson.

"Everybody in the office," Matun replies.

"Okay. I didn't have anything to do with that. In fact, I told Matun and Ta'Tanisha and my daughter, why don't you all give the speeches? Why do you all need me to give speeches? What, are you all handicapped? And no one teach me to give a speech. You are going to tell what happened, what you have done. So why do you all feel so handicapped?"

He had already taken himself out of the picture, out of the equation, and out of the lecture circuit. All news to me.

CHAPTER TWO

On Matters of Race

Born in Trinidad and Tobago, Matun manages Sebi's Los Angeles company, Dr. Sebi's Office LLC. She took time off to travel to Honduras to help Sebi host his visit with me. By the time I meet her in 2005, she and Sebi have been together since the mid-1980s, when she initially worked as his assistant. They have a daughter named Xave, born in 1984 in Puerto Rico, Sebi's home base when he operated The Fig Tree. Matun's a middle-aged woman—late 40s, early 50s—her gray hair a giveaway. She could dye it and pass for a thirty-five-year-old, but like Sebi she's a naturalist comfortable in her smooth brown skin and gray hair. The week we're together in Honduras, Matun's short, trimmed Afro complements the clothes she wears: a sleeveless green floral cotton dress, calf-length; a long-sleeved collared white blouse with a shirtwaist that rests on top of slightly bell-bottomed jeans that hug her slender, curvy hips; T-shirts and airy cotton skirts. She's a silent and reserved Pan-Africanist, with hawk-eyed attention to my interview with Sebi. Once in a while, when the conversation strays from Sebi's biography, she jumps in to defend Sebi's statements about food, race, and Africa.

After we finish a lunch of spelt pasta and vegetables in Sebi's cabin one afternoon, we have a conversation about spirituality and running a business. Spirituality is one of those words that gets a brush of the hand from Sebi but we discuss it anyway. When business comes up, I notice his fiery and highly demonstrative telling of a story about poor women in India and how they improved their lot in life, progressing from a state of disease to ease.

"Let me show her about what we know about Bangladesh," he says to Matun. "They had a group of women who make baskets."

"Yes," I say. I sense his urge to make a point.

"They make baskets, same baskets you see around, making baskets. And then they were so proficient in making these baskets, everybody started buying their baskets. And then one entrepreneur came and saw where he could take their baskets and take it to where? Belgium, and sell them because they were colorful, all kinds of weaves. So the women got together one day and said, 'Let's go to the bank and see if they will lend us some money.' But the world is constructed around a principle: if you're poor, you stay poor. And that's in America too. If you go to America and you try to get money from a bank, 'Uh, what's your credit history?' 'Uh oh. I don't have any.' Well, the women didn't have any credit history, and they went five times to five different banks. But the women, in the last try, there's a man inside there. And he heard the women talk to the manager and what they have done in the past, the other banks they visited, and were refused. The man said,

'What y'all want the money for?'

They said, 'We want to make baskets.'

The man say, 'How much could you pay back every month?'

'We could pay so much every month.'
The man said, 'I will let you have $100,000.' And they start the fuckin' business."

"Ah," I say, trying to lessen his tirade.

"Wait! So the women started paying the man. They paid the man, right?"

"Paid him off," Matun adds.

"Wait, and—"

"And they kept paying and paying," she continues.

"and what happened in twenty years?" Sebi demands.

"They had their own bank!" they shout together.

"American black people don't think like that!" he snaps. "They got their own bank! These twenty women! God damn it, that wasn't on welfare! Our women are on welfare so their creativity is gone. That's what I'm talking about! They got a bank now! They lend money."

"Unaware we sacrifice our children for that welfare," Matun says, with a tone that brings the conversation down a decibel or two.

"That's why I didn't send my children to school. Because these women didn't go to school. See, we could do it," Sebi urges with calm. "Look, these women, Matun and Maa, bought this [*Usha Village*] and that big property up on the hill, and they have a business for twenty years. Two women and me. Two women and me."

As far back as I can remember, Sebi has consistently used what he had overcome physically, mentally, and financially as an example of what others could do to heal themselves in the same areas. I sensed his own perseverance and independence influenced this heated story.

"And they got forty million Blacks. Oh my God," he continues. "They got twenty women in Bangladesh own banks now, their own bank. They lend money to poor people. That's the way you do it!"

Code of Ethics and Race

Sebi's in his element one morning talking about African influences on his life. But a country that gets a verbal spanking for making the black race look bad is Nigeria. He chastises the country for its shady business dealings like a father chastising his son.

"I'm saying that the situation is well confounded due to malnutrition. The African black man, he doesn't want to hear anything about any black man from any other country unless you bring some dollars to invest, and he's going to get the lion share of your investment. That's throughout Africa, not to mention Nigeria. Nigeria made me look bad when I went to Asia because they asked me if I was a Nigerian. I said, 'Why you ask me that?' 'Because if you were Nigerian, we would not do business with you. Because you all are unethical.' That's the mark that the black man has made on his own race. Chinese doesn't go around the world doing that, and if he does that, he does it with protocol, sneaky but decent. You understand? You see, because there is no, what, what, what do you call it? We have no moral code. Yes."

"Code of ethics," Matun offers.

"No moral code or code of ethics among the black race. You can do anything, and you don't have to give account to nobody. But I had to give account to Latin America, yes. Because the communities are breaking down into small principalities, and you're going to live in one of those principalities. And you behave bad, you're in trouble wherever you go. But in America, I could offend the black race in New York and all I have to do is move to L.A. and so what? It's there. That's the way you all live. You all don't live like a village. And I'm not saying that's the fault of black America either. That's the way it is. When I went to America, I could hear the opposition. I was told, 'Why don't you go back to Jumaica? (This is exactly what Sebi said—Jumaica.) You eat monkey hips and grits.' I heard that but I thought it was funny because I'm not a Jumaican."

Yet, through all the prejudice and discrimination he experienced from his own race, Sebi devoted his work to healing it. He held on, just as his great-great-grandmother Elizabeth held on to Violet in the flood of 1925.

"I was one that was taken in by you," he says, recalling his early days in the US, "because my cousin lived with a black American woman named Miriam Jennings. And because of her, I was able to interrelate with black Americans only. And then I became a Black Muslim. That even take it even deeper. But the thing that had me as a Black Muslim was this. There was a thing in which we had to hate white people or the devil. You know, I don't hate the devil. I cannot hate the devil. I can't hate an ant. I cannot hate anything because to hate something, you have to live in a position or in an environment of hate. For you to afford hate you have to live in the environment of hate. And when you live in the environment of hate, it is stressful. And stress is supported by adrenalin. Adrenalin flows when there is stress. But adrenalin, if it flows too much, it poisons the system. So you see, when you hate, you're drinking your own poison. I was never of the opinion of begging the white man for anything or hating the white man for anything. I lived a life in which I provide myself the things that I need.

"But, like we know, everything is in divine order, right? Well, if everything is in divine order, this message also fits within that description. This must be in divine order because we know it now. But the people of fifty years or a hundred years ago didn't know that when they put hog maws in their mouths, they were poisoning themselves. They didn't know that. But how do we know it now? Because it was supposed to be known now. It was in the air. It was there all the time but nobody extrapolated it. No one reached—well you don't even know where to reach, because the information we have to cure AIDS, which is minor, it didn't come out of a book because if it was in a book, then all you need to do is go and buy the book and begin to do exercises, and do it. But it's not in a book. It came out of a vibration, a resonance, something that we black people have yet to understand. We have to understand mechanics not resonance. We do not relate to resonance. We relate to A, B, C and 1, 2, 3, then come Socrates and philosophy. But reality? No. We can't relate to that. So, Sebi, not having the philosophy and the 1, 2, 3, well, all he had to his avail was what Mother Nature had to offer, and that is where I am satisfied. And I learned from that particular perspective what I know."

Race and Resonance Matter—Resonance More

From 1991 to 1994, I worked at National Public Radio on a series it co-produced with the Smithsonian Institution, *Wade in the Water: African American Sacred Music Traditions*. Some days, on my lunch break, I'd leave NPR's M Street N.W. building to go to a bookstore around the corner. I vaguely remember the name. I think it was either Common Concerns or Second Story Books. To this day, I don't know what sent me to that bookstore or why I browsed the section on Eastern religions and stayed there my entire lunch hour. Still in research mode, maybe? I did some of that for the series. But Eastern religions had no direct connection to *Wade in the Water*, a series steeped in African American spirituals and Christian music.

ON MATTERS OF RACE

One day, *The Tibetan Book of Living and Dying* by Sogyal Rinpoche caught my eye and joined me at the cash register. Reading it put me on a path of rebirth and an awareness of life I never had, but it would take years for me to fully grasp and act on what the book imparted. On page 12, Sogyal Rinpoche wrote:

> You will be guided, stage by stage, through the unfolding vision of the journey through life and death. Our exploration necessarily begins with a direct reflection on what death means and the many facets of the truth of impermanence—the kind of reflection that can enable us to make rich use of this life while we still have time, and ensure that when we die it will be without remorse or self-recrimination at having wasted our lives.

It's a thick book I've yet to finish. Every now and then I read random chapters of it because I'm eternally grateful for Sogyal Rinpoche's teachings and the doors he opened, such as books I read by Deepak Chopra, Thich Nhat Hanh, and Maharishi Mahesh Yogi. Of all these enlightened men, Deepak Chopra's name surfaces when Sebi and I talk about divine order and spirituality and how each one affects behavior. Divine order resonates with Sebi, spirituality not so much, as you'll see in the following passage. Sebi respects my feelings about Chopra; on the other hand, he defends his position that resonance trumps the spiritual.

SEBI: Everybody else is spiritual. And I want to be spiritual too. Of course I do, because everybody else claim that they are. Well, if they are spiritual, and I am the child of God, and I have the same components as everyone else, what precludes me in being spiritual? I don't know. But it must be something very sacred. It must be something very, very deep in the spirits, because I cannot find it. And I will not, and I will never afford from my mouth a word that signifies something that I don't know about. Because then I'm lying. I don't know. So I had to take the position, compelled by truth, I don't know what it is to be spiritual, because I don't know. And when I hear people talk about it, they give me their individual interpretation of what it is. Then I know that there is a problem. So I make it very easy. I don't know, and I don't think that I need to know, because I know what keeps me well are the minerals that my body ingests to keep my body strong, not a belief in my skull. Because my belief is predicated by what I eat.

BEVERLY: It is, but Deepak Chopra, I have to really support Deepak Chopra because—

SEBI: Oh, you can support him. All I'm saying—

BEVERLY: I like his readings, I mean I—

SEBI: Now, hold it. You can support Deepak Chopra, and you can support the Dalai Lama. I'm saying, where do we put it into the equation of making life better? That's all I'm asking.

BEVERLY: It helps me see better. Deepak Chopra is a man to help you see that. Food is very important, but—

SEBI: Hold it.

BEVERLY: Deepak Chopra to me, is helping us see. Well, I've always felt it, but he is helping me solidify the notion that the universe really drives and controls and gives us that code of life.

SEBI: The gorilla knows that.

BEVERLY: The code of behavior.

SEBI: The gorilla knows that.

BEVERLY: Well, that's fine but—

SEBI: So what I'm saying—

BEVERLY: Deepak Chopra is trying to get you back to—
SEBI: To what?
BEVERLY: Get you back to that code of behavior.
SEBI: He made a mistake.
BEVERLY: To honor that code.
SEBI: He made a mistake.
BEVERLY: He's trying to get you back to that.
SEBI: Well, I'll tell you what, I am going to talk about Deepak Chopra now, and I want it written. If Deepak Chopra understood cosmic procession—
MATUN: Exactly.
SEBI: He would not take the position as an Indian to talk to the resonance of an African. Why? Because the message is different, just like the medicine and the food. And that happens for every plant, animal, and man. That's the thing that I'm talking about, that you or all of the people that believe in him is like a black man listening to a Chinese.
BEVERLY: But, okay
SEBI: Yeah, you see.
BEVERLY: This is my belief, Sebi.
Sebi: But no!
BEVERLY: Hear, hear.
SEBI: I don't want your belief. I want what you know.
BEVERLY: Okay, this is what I know.
SEBI: Okay.
BEVERLY: This is what I know. I am a species or an entity that is a part of a vast and wonderful universe. I'm a part of this universe.
SEBI: But connected to one gene group.
BEVERLY: Well, I—
SEBI: You don't find zebras—

BEVERLY: I'm a descendant from Africa.

SEBI: Okay, so therefore your message has to come from where?

BEVERLY: Africa.

SEBI: Thank you very much. Now, Deepak Chopra is from where?

BEVERLY: He's from India.

SEBI: Well, thank you very much. So his resonance is different, and therefore, whatever he got to offer, it would be best if he takes it back to India, because there he got more work than here, because they are the most confused. So he's a traitor to his own people.

BEVERLY: Sebi, come on now. Hear me out.

SEBI: No. That is the truth.

BEVERLY: Well, yeah.

SEBI: Because he's an Indian, right? His resonance is different. Deepak Chopra cannot relate to a black person. Why? Deepak Chopra doesn't even know the food of a black man because Deepak Chopra is eating the food of the European himself. Thank you very much.

BEVERLY: Yeah.

SEBI: Wait. I'll be right back. [*Sebi steps outside for a moment to speak to his groundskeeper.*]

BEVERLY: Okay.

SEBI: [*Sebi returns. We continue.*] Because we know that they do not have the amount of carbon that black people have. And they admit to that. They will tell you that. A coach came on the other day and said if you want to win, you have to have black players on your team. Well, why? Why do we run faster? Why are we so rhythmic? Why? See, these questions were never asked. You know something, when I went before the Supreme Court, I said I'm gonna ask a question to see how valuable this question could be because it seems as if black America has been put to sleep forever. The judge said,

'Mr. Alfredo Bowman, the FDA does not want you to disseminate your products.'

I said, 'The FDA is 100 percent right, providing that they could tell us when they removed the black man from Africa, did they bring our food with us Your Honor?'

The judge said, 'No.'

'Well now, the FDA should be qualified to tell us what is the food of the black man that resonates with his cellular predisposition?'

The judge looked at me, and they knew that this was the first time in the history of America that a black man is gonna ask such a question. But it didn't mean anything to black America. I defended them. I defended you in the courts, establishing a medicine that was black, and that could help the whole entire world because it does do the work. It does the work that it was designed to do. And it was proven clinically. It was proven scientifically. It was proven on every level of endeavor.

BEVERLY: Okay, I understand that but when Deepak—and I don't want to spend too much time on Deepak Chopra because he's not the focus of this book—but Deepak Chopra has said many times in his book that if there's an archetype from wherever you are, that you believe in, or there's an entity that you pray to or want to connect with, choose that archetype. He doesn't come with a message that's exclusively East Indian.

SEBI: Do you believe that's the first time I've heard gurus and people like Deepak Chopra? They been coming to America for the last fifty years you know.

BEVERLY: Right.

SEBI: And have conditions changed? They've gotten worse in the last twenty years.

BEVERLY: It changes for people who want change.

SEBI: Well hold it. I'm saying, you see, if it changes for people who want change then we don't need Deepak Chopra. Doesn't make sense, does it? It does not make sense. I'm saying that men like Deepak Chopra are many. They've got them in Europe. Bhagwan Rajneesh was here.[1] He has fifty-two Rolls-Royces.[2] But how did he affect human life? No way. The poor remain poor. The sick remain sick. Deepak Chopra himself wearing glasses. So, all this I see. You understand? And I'm older than the man who talks about spirituality. And in fact, I'm going to talk about that because spiritual people use a word trying to intimidate others as if they have reached a level of understanding that now provides you with the peace and serenity. Not so. Every spiritual person that claim that they are eats garbage. And the garbage dictates and undermines the goal that you pursue. Nobody is going to take that away from Dr. Sebi because he knows that what goes in your colon affects what you think.

BEVERLY: Okay.

SEBI: That goes into any science, on any level of biochemistry. Because I said, I tried to show you, I didn't go to school. Well, how did I arrive at this? And the people who read the books didn't? And why was it when the lady was sick with her, with uh—

BEVERLY: Lockjaw?

SEBI: Lockjaw. Where did I go and get the piece of information? Ah-h, black people in America would say, "That is strange." But they didn't say it was strange when the beaver builds its dam. You see, it's strange then. It's a natural, cosmic arrangement or connection. When you are cosmically connected—the Maya showed us that.[3] The Maya built pyramids that the engineers who went to school cannot build.[4] The black man built pyramids that those of you who went to school cannot build today. So where did they get that from? You see, but we are not thinking. This is why my wife said when glucose has been introduced to the body, it does something very strange to the hypothalamus gland, which is the gland that processes information. Now, what are we talking about now? Information that everybody had at one point in history. But because we were removed from our mother, we're all confused. When the information comes back, we want to put that information against others. But you can't do that because you don't even know the information of our mothers and fathers. We don't even know that. But the little that Dr. Sebi held onto, look what he's doing. He has healed many people of sickle cell anemia that they said is incurable, AIDS, lupus, and blindness, not to mention diabetes. So, if with the little attention Dr. Sebi give to the African perspective, I'm quite sure there is nobody in India that has accomplished that. But the African has. But we don't want to accept that because the hypothalamus gland is working. It's doing its job. What I have done and other black men in America have done, there's nobody in India or Japan that has accomplished that. Nowhere in the world. And I know that, and I can substantiate that, you see. But we are not in favor of ourselves now. But I, Dr. Sebi, said one day if I'm the only individual on the planet that defends Mother Africa, all the way, unadulterated—I didn't go to Egypt to get anything. Why? What is in Egypt but a bunch of stones? And you come back [*Not Beverly per se*],

'Oh, I visited Karnak and I went into the tombs of Hatshepsut. I went into the tomb of Ramses II. When I went to Giza I went to the Pyramids.'

'Ok, fine. You came back, right? How much money did you spend?'

'$3,000.'

And you came back and you tell me about these stones. Fine. I didn't go to Egypt. I went to the jungles of Africa, and I came back with an herb call cancansa that cured a man in L.A. of prostate cancer. And you came back from Egypt with nothing. That's what I'm talking about. To be useful.

BEVERLY: Yes.

SEBI: Not to talk about philosophy. No. That has no place in life. Life has no place for philosophy. You eat. You sleep. And you shelter, then you die. But there's no place for philosophy. Where does it fit? Now, an African man showed me something once, and when you put it into the sequence of things, you're going to see the beauty of this thing. He tells me,

'Is it a fact that we talk about riches and diamonds and gold?'

I said yes.

He said, 'Isn't that something, that the diamonds and the gold were always in Africa but we were living without it. It was just there. It was doing what it was supposed to be doing.'

Conveying resonance from one point to another because gold is an electrical conductor, the best in the world.

'But since,' he said, 'Dr. Sebi, civilized man came and took it out of the ground and then put it on your skin, that's an oxide. It's going to burn your cells.' He said, 'Furthermore, how did we live in Africa without the gold, without the diamonds, without all of that? We were living, right Dr. Sebi?'

I said, 'Yes sir.'

He said, 'Can we go back to that again?'

I said, 'Well there are some people that need gold and diamond on their body.'

He said, 'Well, we know that.'

'But you know why they are doing that. They are conditioned.'

He said, 'Are you one of them?'

I said, 'I don't even wear a wristwatch.'

BEVERLY: But wait a minute. You said gold is not good to wear?

SEBI: Whenever you take—

BEVERLY: They have placed a value on gold. I mean thousands, millions of dollars on gold.

MATUN: I used to be an electrician.

BEVERLY: Oh, please, please, yes, let her talk.

MATUN: The best conductor is gold for electricity.

SEBI: The planet uses it for conducting electricity because the planet is alive. The planet needs the oil. It needs the gold. It needs the silver. It needs the opium. It needs the iron. It needs everything your body needs—

BEVERLY: Yes.

SEBI: To function.

MATUN: And the diamonds.

SEBI: And the diamonds. But since we are civilized, and we need to be held by our hands, we need to be told what to do and what not to do by other people who call themselves leaders, well then you become vulnerable. Me, I prefer to make the decision for Sebi. I, Sebi, have been doing that all his life. From the age of eight I have made decisions for me, not someone making it for me or telling where I should look. No. I'm an individual. How can any leader stand up in front of an audience without understanding that everybody in front of him is uniquely different, unlike the other? The resonance of one, not so for the other. So how could you have a message for all? That is downright stupidity. I want it to be written like that, because that's what it is. All of us resonate on a different vibration. So how can I have a message for you? The only reason you're looking for a message outside of yourself because you've been undermined. Repeating again, undermined by glucose. When the glucose has been removed, everything that I'm telling you to do, you can see even better, without someone telling you anything. Because who told me to be a healer? Who teach me to be a healer? Who teach me to be a steam engineer? I didn't go to school for steam engineering. I didn't go to school to be a healer and to understand the science of biochemistry. You see, but because we've been so compromised, we think everybody needs to do that. No, no, no, no, no, not everybody needs to go to school. No way. Our daughter showed that. All of my daughters didn't go to school, and they manage the business. How come they can do that? You see, I put the black gene to a test, like many have not. And I know what the black gene can do, without the aid of this thing they call education. My daughters did it, and my son, and they bad. They tougher than Dad, because one day Sesa took a glass with some water in it. He said,

'Dad, you made a statement that everything that has life must necessarily have cells.'

I said, 'Yes. Without cells there could be no life.'

He said, 'Oh yeah? Well, let me see.'

So he picked up a glass of water. It was in the river, and he put the glass in front of me and he said,

'Now, is water alive Dad?'

I said yes.

'Does it have cells?'

Remember, I could see through it. I said, 'Yes it has cells.'

'What are they?'

'They are electrons.'

He said, 'Damn it, that's the only answer you could have given me.'

BEVERLY: [*I chuckle*] It's the right answer?

SEBI: I got him though.

BEVERLY: It's the right answer?

SEBI: Sure. Sure it was, and he knew it.

BEVERLY: Okay.

SEBI: But no one ever asked me that question. It goes by people. People only know what comes out of a book. But life does not come out of a book. It came out of a life sequence, a life structure, a cosmic arrangement. Food begins to show us a whole lot of things that was never before treated, because nobody came to tell us that we could not eat rice and beans and that we shouldn't put blood in our mouth. Nobody came with that message. But we found it. So how did we get the message? There again, the same way that the eagle got the message to make its nest.

BEVERLY: From the cosmic—

SEBI: From the cosmic arrangement of things.

BEVERLY: From that vibration.

SEBI: From that vibration, you see. Because if we had continued to eat the food that our mothers and fathers ate in the forest of Africa, we would not be at each other's throat today, because we were not living that way when we were in the forest. And then, all these dialects. What did we speak? What was our language? We know we didn't speak those dialects that they are speaking now. So what did we speak? We didn't have any dictionary. We were so tough we didn't have any dictionary to communicate. But now, homo sapiens need a dictionary and need someone to decipher it for them and teach them how to talk, how to speak. Oh my God. Look at the handicap. You gonna teach me how to eat also. You're going to teach me how to worship God. You have to teach. Well, what happened to me? What happened to the me? What did you do to it? And how damaged is the me that I'm unaware of? Because if I have to be taught how to eat, I have to be taught how to sleep, how many hours to sleep, something is wrong. Something is drastically wrong. So what do we do?

BEVERLY: To reverse it. We must reverse what we're going through?

SEBI: Well, that is the intent, to help, to reverse the conditioning. But to reverse the conditioning, we have to remove what brought the conditioning in the first place.

Dis-Ease

American Negroes and Africa
Source: W. E. Burghardt Dubois, *The World and Africa*

When the Cotton Kingdom of the 19th century built on black slavery led to a campaign in church and society to discount Africa, its culture and history, American Negroes shrank from any ties with Africa and accepted in part the color line.

Ease

Chapter 7: Food and the African Gene
Source: Dr. Sebi, *Sojourn to Honduras Sojourn to Healing*

The African people lived for millions of years without the aid of money. Now the African people find themselves needing money to feed themselves…We came from a people that didn't have any money. We could live life without money. We could design societies. All it takes is some mud and some grass and we could build empires again. Because we did it right here in Usha Village. All these huts are mud. They're mud and grass. And we could do it again as easy as that.

CHAPTER THREE

On Matters of Culture

New Orleans in 1954 is a segregated port city, a white, Creole, and brown town plastered with signs that remind folks how to behave: Colored Entrance, White Entrance, Colored Waiting Room, Whites Only, Colored Water Fountain. When twenty-year-old Dr. Sebi settles down there in those days, he's Alfredo Bowman, merchant seaman, transporter of cargo and travelers. He's tall, jovial, and amazed at all the welcoming colored people wherever he goes, including Tremé, the oldest black neighborhood in America. Two-hundred-year-old Congo Square fascinates him too, that historic gathering and marketplace for enslaved and free Africans, including West African blacksmiths and wrought iron artisans who built the balconies and rails in the French Quarter. In *Negro Art: Past and Present*, Dr. Alain Locke writes, "The most authentic tracing of any considerable school of master craftsmen has been in the connection with the famous Negro blacksmiths of New Orleans who furnished the hand-wrought iron grilles that ornamented the balconies and step balustrades of the more pretentious homes."

This migration of ancestral skill—African blacksmithing is over one thousand years old—demonstrates divine order at its best, that natural progression of life Sebi encouraged. It shows a cosmic arrangement, a continuum that modern man can use to navigate life.

"You know what, I'm going to tell you something about government and culture," Sebi says. "Do you know that culture supersedes government?"

"Culture supersedes government?" I ask.

"That's right. Black America doesn't know that they have rights and that they could take out of their culture components that would improve the quality of their lives. They, black America, doesn't know these things. But if you ask black America about the Fourteenth Dynasty in Egypt, they know all about that. If you ask them about the wars in Songhay, they know all about that too. They can tell you all about the things that they read in those books, but when it comes down to what, to the components that would enrich their lives, to bring about something better—comfort—black America doesn't know any of those components. Because there is a healer in black America that brought us soybean and sodium. Instead of complementing, he was affecting the lymphatic system of the black race, not to mention the blood and the bones. But, like I said, a one-eyed man is king where everybody's blind. So, this healer brought us sodium and soybean in the name of health."

"What was his name?"

"Well, we don't have to bring his name or talk about his name. But those who bought the product know that on the very label it said sodium and soy, soy and sodium. That is the extent of our understanding about foods."

It's a gradual process to learn what healthy food is. I didn't know the effects of soy until after I researched what Sebi said about it. As usual, he was right, but the revelation shocked me to the core. Chai tea latte is one of my favorite drinks. I'd been drinking it with soy milk for five years, thinking I was a good former asthmatic for giving up cow's milk. But when I learned that soy contains phytoestrogen, an endocrine disruptor, I switched to coconut milk posthaste. Endocrine disruptor? Yes, one of the reasons why Sebi wanted us to stop consuming it.

According to the U.S. National Institutes of Health and the U.S. Environmental Protection Agency, endocrine disruptors like phytoestrogen found in soybeans "alter the structure or function(s) of the endocrine system and cause adverse effects." And the adverse effects are? Disruption of lactation, the timing of puberty, the inability to produce viable, fertile offspring, sex specific behavior, premature and compromised fertility. And not only that. Consuming soy can cause hypothyroidism and increase estrogen levels in men.[1] And consider GMOs. The U.S. Department of Agriculture said 94 percent of soybean farmland in the U.S. was used to grow genetically engineered soybeans in 2014.

Despite all that, Sebi was well aware that emotional, generational, and even financial reasons called for a gradual, instead of a cold turkey, leap to healthy eating. But he wanted us to make the leap just the same.

Dr. Frances Cress Welsing

Every now and then, I notice Sebi praises someone who shares his point of view about race, culture, and identity, even if the person is trained in psychology, one of the sciences he occasionally rebukes in his lectures. Dr. Frances Cress Welsing, psychiatrist and Afrocentrist, is the woman. Sebi said "She came through like a champ" on a radio program he listened to in Los Angeles. I know Dr. Welsing's work and her sister Lorne Cress Love. When I was a student at Howard University, I interned with Love at WPFW radio in Washington, D.C. She served as news and community affairs director.

Sebi approves of the steps Dr. Welsing recommended Blacks take to improve their place in America. When he says the behavior involves honesty and a code of ethics, I ask him how that relates to culture. He sheds his healer cloak and dons that of a professor. His voice is clear and robust above the volume of the television chatter in the background when he explains that culture, your ancestral culture, is your origin.

"You can't say that what you acquire later is your culture," he says. "No. Your culture is your origin. It comes out of the origin, that which was arranged by nature. That which you live."

"That which your ancestors lived," I repeat for clarity.

"That which was arranged by nature. That's how culture comes about. But now, we don't have anything to say 'this is ours.' And anytime one of us violates that code of ethics that is part of our culture, then we know that we have a violator on our hands. But as for now, we have no violators. Everybody can do anything. They can do anything. You know, we can act in any manner. It doesn't matter. We could lie. We could steal. The other day, Dr. Frances Cress Welsing was on the program, which is known in Los Angeles as *Front Page*. I was on *Front Page* the day before Dr. Frances Cress Welsing was on there. And I listened to this sister. I listened very, very, very, very intensely. Because I do respect her judgment. Certain things I disagree with, like certain things I disagree with a whole lot of people. And I guess a whole lot of people disagree with certain things with me. But the essence of the woman, the essence of what she

ON MATTERS OF CULTURE

was saying is what I was concerned with. And she came through like a champ. She said, this is the essence of what she said. Since there is no code of ethics that we could, say, identify and relate to, well, let us do this. Let's stop lying. Stop stealing. She went on with all of the things that she mentioned that we should not do. But lying and stealing are two things she emphasized we should not do. That, I think, was the best thing I've heard in fifty-two years that I've been in America."

"But what does that have to do with culture?" I ask.

"Because that came out of our culture. There was nothing to steal. We acquired that here. We have something to steal now, but when we were home everybody was naked. Everybody ate from the same tree. There was nothing to steal. Steal was not even in our vocabulary, not to mention the act itself. What are you going to steal? We all are naked. There's nothing to steal. Now we're stealing. And we're lying. And we're killing. Did that happen then? No. What am I going to kill my neighbor for? So she was right. We should stop it. And we are notorious liars. And we cheat and we lie so easily, and then we do things to each other and think that it should be accepted as passé. No. Look, I had brothers to ask me for my formulas. I had brothers to put my money in their name in the bank in D.C. That's right. You see, not to mention many other people in New York, who I had healed of diseases and worked for me and took the money out of the bank and said it was theirs. All this happened to me. But I understood why. What about the woman's son that came from Buffalo, New York, to kill me? Only because he thought his mother was too close to me. He came to kill me. But instead, a truck killed him. Right here. I had to bury him. Right here in Honduras I buried him. His mother told me to bury him here. So I know what to expect from black America. I know what to expect, because I know what they gave us to eat. And the result of that which they gave us to eat would precipitate these acts."

His tragic tales shock and disappoint me. I keep it inside. No need to rile him. Besides, his memories have already succeeded. So I ask him a question about culture with as much diplomacy as I can. "Do you believe we've taken on a culture of someone else? That's why we're in the condition we're in today as a people?"

"I don't believe in anything," he states with conviction. "And I don't live in the world of belief. I know that we took on another culture. Look at the language we're speaking right now. Is that African?"

"No."

"The clothes we're wearing, is that African?"

"No."

"The food we're eating, is it African?"

"No."

"So have we taken on what? Another culture? We only know the other culture. We don't know ours, because if we knew ours, our women wouldn't straighten their hair. She would know the value of it. Our women wouldn't put no lipstick on her lips because she would know that lead is poisonous. We no longer live in the village. So we cannot keep tabs or monitor the behavior of those who are a part of this village. Like I said earlier, I could offend in one village. I could offend in New York and I could go to L.A. But if you offend in a village and you have to go to another, they're going to ask you why you left, and they're going to investigate why you left. That's right. They want to know. That's why you have to behave yourself. And this is what Frances, Dr. Frances Cress Welsing, was showing us. We have no code of ethics. We could do anything. So we have no boundaries. So this healing that is being afforded to the world came out of that culture, because if it had come from any other, what race is doing what we're doing? None. So therefore, it is African, as they call it. And I doubt whether I should, in the future, I doubt whether I would be using that word African too. Because that word African isn't ours. That also is a European word."

"So what would you call us then?"

"Why call us anything?"

"Okay. Labels again."

"Why have names? Not only do we have names, we have a Social Security number. But is that a part of our culture? No. Was it part of our culture to eat blood? No. Was it part of our culture to drink cow milk? No. We drink our mother's breast. That was all we needed because there is an intelligence in that milk. And I have experience with my own children and others who drink their mother's breast. They didn't go to school, but they could think. You see we equate school with thinking. Well, if school is equated with thinking or thinking equated with school, well, just visit the Maya. Did he have schools? Well, how come he build those pyramids? Okay," Sebi ends with emphasis.

He's gone back to preslavery, precolonial days again, a simpler, independent time when tribes commingled and bartered. I wondered how to parlay that experience into current times, now that habitats are far less rural than a thousand years ago.

"A lot of us don't live like you live," I say. "You live in this very beautiful, very lush tropical environment. You have a lot of land here. And you've used your skill to create Usha Village. But how do we use what you've used in a city? Or a place like the United States, or a city in Jamaica like Kingston or any other city where you have a lot of black people? How do we bring a thousand-year-old existence into today's times and conditions?"

"You can't," he says, plain and simple.

"I mean, the times are different."

"You can't do that in a city but you can do it in a forest," he insists.

"We don't all live in a forest."

"Hey, but I live in the forest."

"Not all of us do. The majority of us, the majority of us of African descent, we live in cities."

"Well, it's not going to be done."

"But we can still be healed where we live, right? Right where we are." I refuse to let him exile city dwellers.

"Not as effective as you would in a forest. But you'll be healed because I healed many people that live in the cities. Sure, of course you'll heal," he relents. "But I'm saying, to live, we could go back to the forest. Like we intend to do a model in Guinea. We're going to Guinea to do a model. We're going to show the world that you could live in the forest better than any millionaire. And you would live in peace and self-subsistence. The water we're going to drink, it's thermal. The water we're going to bathe in is thermal. And the same thermal water we use for what? Irrigation. And we're going to grow our food. What are the foods we are going to grow? Well, we're going to grow only natural foods. And, in the meantime, until the food is growing, we could go and get the roots from the plants, the herbs. And we could nourish ourselves for ninety days until the crop comes. And about clothes, that's easy. Just grow the cotton because we got five thousand acres of land given to us. We can grow all the cotton in the world. And to nourish the cotton, to ensure a good crop, well, it would be done organic. Electric agriculture will be put in place. So we have our cotton clothes, and we have our brick-laid environment because we're going to make our brick from the red mud, the same mud we use to make our houses, and we do it exactly the way you see it here."

ON MATTERS OF CULTURE

"At Usha Village," I say.

"That's right, very pretty," he boasts with wide eyes, his chest out, and a bit of a fidget in his body that this talk about sustainable natural environments causes. "And you lay back now. Everybody is laid back in their cotton gowns. They don't have to go to the supermarket. They don't have to definitely go to the doctor. And, we just lay back and enjoy. But that, in America, is wishful thinking. But I want to let America know, it is not an impossibility. Because I'm doing it right here in Honduras, right here at this village. I don't need to leave my village to go anywhere to get anything. It's right here."

"That's true. I've tasted the almonds here."

"You see. It's easy. But black America isn't looking for comfort. They are looking for the bling-bling. Not comfort. The bling-bling doesn't bring comfort. So if you're going to have all those things on your body, well, you cannot live in a natural village that perpetuates life itself, self-subsistence. It could be done, because water is the base and then food. The clothing, we could do that. Just grow cotton. And we could spin cotton. We could make the best cotton clothes in the world, right? We always have. And me, you know what it is to wear cotton gowns in your environment, where you don't even have to cook food anymore? What you talkin' about? And then you gonna tell me that I have to leave that and go to New York to punch a clock. Oh yeah, okay. Hm-m. And then you're going to offer $100,000 a year. But the stress that comes with making $100,000 a year is what I'm not willing to acquire or accept. No. Life is worth more than any money because all my friends that pursued money, including Kirby, Kirby Brown, yeah. Kirby Brown. We were twelve. Kirby and I were Seven-Day Adventist for one day or two. But I had to recite in the thirteenth sabbath, and I was going home. I say,

'Kirby, how you like the sermon?'

He said, 'Man, they talk about Solomon. I don't like that shit. I want money.'

I said, 'Well, I agree with Solomon, you know. He could solve problems. I like that. I like understanding.'

He said, 'Well, you go for that. I want money.'

"Kirby died eleven years ago. He became a cab driver in New York. And the very thing that I pursued is responsible for me being here. I pursued understanding. And in that understanding, in the pursuit of understanding, I found health. And it has me laughing now and being happy, doing all kinds of acrobatic stupidness. But I like it because I can act stupid again and enjoy it. That's why the children come around here and they don't want to leave, because they found a grownup that is as stupid as they are. And they enjoy that, and I enjoy it too because they accept me as their peer. But when I go around the people who are my age, seventy plus, all I hear is a sad story. And I don't want to hear that."

"What's the story?"

"Well, you know the stories. You know what they are. You know what the stories are. I don't have to go into them."

I want to know. I continue to probe, feeling there's a gem of insight in the answer, no matter how lengthy the response. "About health? About the problems of the world?"

"He's concerned with everything but himself. The last woman that left him. The money he could have had. The job that he lost. Instead of looking at himself and realizing that he's alive."

Anthropology and Human Progression

Sebi's well versed in Egypt's history. I assume his membership in the Nation of Islam when he was a young man in New Orleans helped with this. The Nation of Islam writes and teaches the history of Egypt. So Sebi knows a thing or two about African Americans' knowledge about the country. Needless to say, as we talk about that in his cabin one afternoon, he has strong opinions about the perceived benefit of Egyptian history. He questions whether people apply it to present-day experiences. Vanessa joins us. She's the young English tutor from Brooklyn who studied anthropology in college.

"This is very, very important because this has never been touched upon," he begins. "We talk about Queen Tiye. We talk about Queen Nzinga. We talk about the Songhay period. Oh, we talk about Timbuktu. We talk about Karnak and Abu Simbel. We know all about what went down in the Egyptian Fourteenth Dynasty of Egypt. We know what went down in Egypt. We know all of those things. So the one thing that I noticed, and I ask even the young lady here, Vanessa, the anthropologist. I said am I out of sync if I were to mention that anthropology is the study of cultures and human progression? Yes, I know that. I don't need to go to school to know that. But in their research, in their anthropological research, none of them ever talk about food consistency with gene. Nobody ever talk about that. So those who believe in anthropology and follow it, I'm going to ask them in this book, what did you gain from anthropology that you could firmly apply to improve the condition of our lives right now?"

Sebi often directs the question about pragmatic solutions to today's health, race, and cultural problems to politicians as well as anthropologists. Throughout his tenure as a natural healer, he offered a method—a practical, hands-on method—to reverse diseases like AIDS, sickle cell anemia, leukemia, diabetes, impotence, and fibroid tumors. In September 2002 Sebi requested a meeting with Robert Mugabe, the president of Zimbabwe. In the request—a typed letter—he asked the question, "What can we do to improve the quality of life for our people?"

I'm thrilled to share the eloquent way Sebi answered the question and presented his offer to Zimbabwe. Here are excerpts from that letter, addressed to Dr. Simbi Mubako, ambassador of the Republic of Zimbabwe.

Dear Mr. Mubako:

In 1988, when the USHA Research Institute won its case against the New York State Supreme Court, it was the first victory of its kind. That victory included the right to practice the healing traditions of our forefathers by using herbs and other natural nutritional substances that are consistent with our genetic structure. Our premise and methodology were proven effective and true.

...I would like to take this opportunity to give you a brief synopsis of how our premise and methodology achieve successful results in eradicating diseases.

...According to Western medical research, diseases are a result of the host being infected with a "germ," "virus," or "bacteria." And in their approach in treating these "infestations," inorganic, carcinogenic chemicals are employed. Our research immediately uncovers flaws in their premise and methodology through basic deductive reasoning.

...In contrast, as we examine the African approach to disease, it diametrically opposes the present Western approach. Specifically, the African Bio-mineral Balance refutes the germ/virus/bacteria premise. Our research reveals that all manifestations of disease finds its genesis when and where the mucous membrane has been compromised. For example, if there is excess mucous in the bronchial tubes, the disease is Bronchitis; if it is in the lungs, the disease is Pneumonia; in the pancreatic duct, it is Diabetes; in the joints, Arthritis.

...In the fall of 1988, while explaining this very premise, Dr. Victor Herbert, Head of the Veterans Administration Hospital in New York City inquired, "If the genesis of all disease can be found in the mucous membrane, then what about A.I.D.S.? Is A.I.D.S. mucous too?" The answer is YES. So, where do we find the mucous in Acquired Immune Deficiency Syndrome? The mucous is found in the skin tissue, the blood, and the lymphatic system, otherwise known as the immunological system. In removing the mucous from the immunological system, the USHA Research Institute has been successful in curing not only A.I.D.S., but Sickle cell anemia, Diabetes, Blindness, Impotence, and many other ailments as well.

...In 1988, the Supreme Court of New York State challenged our premise and methodology. The presiding judge, the Honorable Ann Felton [sic] [Anne Feldman], ordered the Institute to present nine patients that had been successfully treated for the diseases the Institute claimed to cure. Seventy-seven patients appeared to testify, including a client who flew in from Italy. Each client was required to bring medical records from accredited medical institutions, indicating the diseases they had prior to receiving treatment from the Institute, including H.I.V./A.I.D.S. cases, no longer existed.

...Through this judicial process, the Supreme Court was made aware of the efficacy of the African Bio Mineral Balance.

...Among the 77 clients that testified in 1988, some were former H.I.V./A.I.D.S. patients. Other H.I.V./A.I.D.S.

patients were proven cured in years to follow, including Oswald Savala (tested by Laboratorio Parades, La Ceiba Honduras, C.A., 1994); Alfredo Lagos (tested by Red Cross Laboratories, Tegucigalpa, Honduras, C.A., 1995); and a client tested by the San Diego County Public Health Laboratory in 1998, who requested anonymity.

...Unlike other therapies, the African Bio-mineral Balance specifically benefits the nutritional needs of the African gene structure. But the beauty of the African Bio-mineral Balance is, because of its highly electrical nature, it has ample capacity to accommodate the nutritional needs of the entire human species. Over the years, we have treated people from all walks of life. In our early years, the bulk of our clientele were Mexican and Caucasian.

...We are proud to say our methodology, though initially designed to rescue the African gene, complements the genealogy of all races.

...All of the African Bio-mineral Balance compounds are comprised of natural plants, which means its constitution is of an alkaline nature. This is important and instrumental in our success in reversing pathologies.

...In addition to removing the accumulation of years of toxins, the African Bio-mineral Balance replaces depleted minerals and rejuvenates damaged cell tissue eroded by the acid, diseased state.

...Because genetics is not addressed in the treatment of disease, the Black race is suffering the most. Whether in Africa or America, the health and well-being of Black people worldwide is being undermined by the same culprit. For example, in my travels to Africa, I noticed the Black female is beset with the same maladies that plague Black women in the United States. They include high anemia and reproductive disorders (i.e., fibroid tumors, vaginitis, yeast infections). Their diseased state also negatively impacts the babies developing in the womb of this "acid flora." Similarly, Black males on both continents share similar ailments (anemia, hypertension, prostate problems, impotence).

...The culprit mentioned earlier is THE DIET. Specifically, we have been conditioned to ingest so called "foods" that create an acid environment in the body.

...Enduring centuries of malnourishment due to the adulteration of our food supply, we have been conditioned to believe corn, wheat, rice, beans, potatoes, millet, cassava, palm oil, carrots, hogs, goats, lambs, cows, chickens, eggs, dairy products and many other toxic artificial substances are not only "food," but are indigenous to the land known as Africa. In our research, we discovered only natural plants—plants made by Nature—are alkaline and do not distress the body when ingested.

...The inevitable question is what can we do to improve the quality of life for our people? The irony is Africa is starving; yet nutrition is at our very feet in the form of natural plants! What is even more ironic—and frightening—is the "humanitarian efforts" to "feed" the starving in Africa are creating yet another catastrophic scenario. "Megahybrid" grains, specifically genetically engineered corn, is being shipped into Africa by the boatloads. Desperate, starving African people are consuming this highly adulterated grain while Western scientists admit the adverse effects of ingesting genetically modified foodstuffs...PLUS, there are deep concerns that the people will resort to planting this genetically altered grain; the results being disastrous—and mostly irreparable—to the ecosystem contaminated by its mutated pollen!

...We must take action. We must save ourselves... Africa is rich with natural resources, and we are a resourceful people.

...Besides being the creator of the African Bio-mineral Balance, I am a Steam Engineer, and have applied my knowledge in botany and biochemistry to horticulture. Utilizing the land on the Usha Healing Village in Honduras, Central America, I have conducted successful horticultural experiments on the effects of natural vegetation cell food in cultivating hearty, bountiful, nutrient-rich fruits and vegetables.

...It would indeed be an honor, and give me great pleasure to be afforded the opportunity to be of assistance to my Brothers and Sisters in Zimbabwe. I humbly request the opportunity to meet with President Robert Mugabe for the purpose of developing and implementing a plan to restore the health and wholeness of your beautiful country, and ultimately, the African continent.

Respectfully yours

Hippocrates Validated African Herbs

Sebi eventually traveled to Zimbabwe. He met the country's public health officials, including Minister of Health and Child Welfare Dr. David Parirenyatwa. But as you might already know, from reading *Seven Days in Usha Village: A Conversation with Dr. Sebi*, the trip turned out bittersweet, with Sebi feeling that since the Parirenyatwa Hospital in Zimbabwe was named after Dr. Parirenyatwa's father, Dr. Tichafa Samuel Parirenyatwa, the public health officials would listen to, but not act on, what Dr. Sebi the herbalist had to offer. On November 7, 2005, inside

Sebi's cabin at Usha Village, he recounts what happened before and during his trip to Zimbabwe.

"We heard there was a situation in Zimbabwe that merits attention. My wife (Matun) and I said look, since Africa is Mother Africa and Zimbabwe is in need, just go there. Just go to Zimbabwe. So she put aside so many thousands of dollars, and I went to Zimbabwe to help them. And when we got there, they put us through a lot of red tape. I understand that too. I didn't mind. Then they say, 'Okay, you're going to get an audience with the minister of health.' I said okay. So I got the audience with the minister of health, Dr. Parirenyatwa. And that's the name of the hospital. Her and I said if this minister of health name is the name of the hospital and his daddy was the first black doctor in southern Rhodesia, we put it together. He's not going to do it. Why would he compromise his position to an herbalist? Regardless if people die."

That state of limbo reared its head again in America, with congressional leaders on Capitol Hill. Sebi often talks about the time in March 2004 when he travelled to Washington, D.C., with singer Michael Jackson to help him and members of the Congressional Black Caucus launch an HIV/AIDS fundraising tour. Ambassadors from several African countries attended: Angola, Cape Verde, Lesotho, Liberia, Madagascar, Malawi, Mali, Mozambique, Niger, Nigeria, Oman, Senegal, Sierra Leone, Swaziland, and Zimbabwe, several of them ravaged by AIDS. Sebi didn't speak at the meeting, but he was certain all the attendees knew about his treatments for AIDS. Even so, instead of acknowledging him, they withheld verbal or other kinds of support. They sidelined him.

"I think you have to be validated. I think with a lot of us, including African Americans—"

"You have to be validated?" Sebi interrupts. "Nobody in the United States has been more validated than Dr. Sebi. He was validated by the Supreme Court to the extent that he is the one that was given the credit to install an institute that is validated by the Supreme Court. Validated! So I have to be validated by a white man for my black brothers to accept me? Well, if that is the thing, they all are going to die. It's as simple as that. It's as simple as that. So validated, validated? Those who have been validated, do they cure anything? So we shouldn't use validation as the premise or as the foundation or as a reason—"

"To accept you," I practically whisper to lessen validation's blow.

"We're not going to do it," Sebi continues. He's wound up. My lowered voice is of no consequence. "I live in a decent place. I live in a nice place. That's it. So the world showed me you don't give a fuck, fine. The world showed me that's where you are, well, that's good with me. But I'm going to be where I'm supposed to be, right? Happy. I brought you a gift and you should be glad. Beyond that point, fuck you. Straight up. Because you have no respect for your mother. The black African people have no respect for their mother, not one country has exhibited that. I'm not talking about I'm sorry because I'm not validated, no. It's not about being validated. Those black African people have no respect for their mother. And I want that in the book."

"Yes, it will be there," I promise.

"Validation. Hippocrates went to Africa to learn the uses of herbs, but they're going to prefer a white perspective above their own mother. Well, that's fine with me. I didn't. I'm cured. But I know for certain that every African leader is impotent.[2] That I know."

"Impotent?"

"He has to be. I know that because we found impotence in Africa at age nineteen, on the average is thirty.³ And those leaders eat cassava that you can't tell them about. Yeah, the African that I learn in my house is not the African I saw when I went to Africa. And I want to read that in this book, because we have got to start defending ourselves against the ruthlessness, against inequity. We hide the inequity that exists in the black family. We hide it. So therefore, it is perpetuated by the leaders. They don't give a damn about what they could do or not do, because they know that you're going to hide it. Because you're going to say, 'Well, you know, uh, you know, you got to give him time, and after all.' Yeah, okay, all these excuses."

It's a contentious moment, and I admit I fanned the flames. I tend to give people the benefit of the doubt. That's why I mentioned validation. Skeptics want proof you can cure the incurable. They want to see your clinical trials, published thesis, or framed degree or seal of approval from the powers that be. Until they see any of that, you're *persona non grata* or, to some skeptics, a quack.

Fifty years after rooting his life in American culture, Sebi has returned to his native home. He's a bit testy one evening in his cabin when he tells me the state of black culture is such that Blacks know more about Egyptian culture than their own West and Central Africa ancestral customs and skills. Even noted historian and sociologist Chancellor Williams, who wrote *The Destruction of Black Civilization*, missed this point in his research, Sebi says, recalling his visit with the scholar in Washington, D.C.

A friend convinced Sebi to go visit Dr. Williams to help restore his vision. But down through the years, Sebi tells me, many of his supporters like his friend (and me) jump at the chance to promote his natural healing without knowing the backlash and turned backs he's experienced.

"Everybody comes to me after others have failed," he says. "So my position is one that is not so secure in the sense that people come to me first. No. They come to me after they had five operations, chemotherapy, about a thousand doses and many tablets. Then they come to me when everything is about to fall apart. 'And Sebi, you better perform. And if you don't perform, you're a liar.' Oh, but then you go to the man, like Chancellor Williams. I'm going to mention Chancellor Williams now, the man that wrote *The Destruction of Black Civilization*, the man who should have showed us what was the cause of the destruction, and what was lost in the destruction. He didn't mention that. So Chancellor Williams, now he is going to be asked a question, that he, I know, went to his grave thinking about it. What was the question? Right in D.C., at the Woodner Apartment. I was taken there by a sister, and I told her, I said, 'Why do you want to take me to this man? This man is a writer. This man is a historian. This man is not a common man. I am a common man. And elite people do not share moments with common people. They just don't do that.' Because women have told me, in California, 'Well, Alfredo, I don't believe that we could have anything in common because I'm educated.' And I agree with her. I said, 'Girl you're right.' So, Chancellor Williams, being that he is the educator, I said to her,

'Why do you believe that he's gonna submit to whatever I have to say?'

'Because of what your history is.'

I said, 'Yeah? Let's go.'

"Because she was just like you, 'Oh no, Oprah gonna do it,'" he mocks, recalling a conversation we had in Los Angeles about pitching an interview on the *Oprah Winfrey Show*. "She said, 'Oh no, Chancellor Williams is gonna do it.' I said just go. So I went. And I went upstairs and I saw the man. I said good morning. It was early in the morning. I said this is the man that's been writing about us. Fine. Well, it's all commerce. It's money. It's a book. Make money, like Alex Haley, *Roots*. It was good. Everybody bought *Roots*. It's a book that you read that something happened. You put it on the shelf. So I said,

'Chancellor Williams, Mr. Williams, I have been, in the past, useful in reversing a disease that I was told you are suffering from. You are losing your sight.'

He said, 'Oh yes. That's true. That's true.'

I said, 'Mr. Williams I have helped many that were blind. After eleven years they're seeing.'

'Oh, but my doctor said that everything's okay. Everything's all right.'

'Mr. Williams, how many years have you been seeing your physician?'

'Oh, he been my physician for twenty-seven years.'

I said, 'But when he first became your physician did you have your sight, completely?'

He said, 'Yes.'

'Well, it became progressively worse later on?'

'Yes.'

'And everything is all right?'

"Well, if Mr. Chancellor Williams, an educator, an historian, an archaeologist, took that position against me without a legitimate excuse, what do you think I expect from the rest of the public?"

In my thoughts I agree with Sebi. I remember a similar experience when I introduced his Eva Salve to an elderly friend with arthritis who lived in the Mount Pleasant neighborhood of Washington, D.C. Emma refused to let it immobilize her for life. Well into her eighties at five foot two inches, Emma ran her own errands with the support of a cane: picking up her prescriptions from the drugstore, buying just enough groceries to fill her lightweight shopping bag, and cooking the food—South Carolina style—when she returned home. She traveled by DC Metro bus with "arther" in tow. When I mentioned how Eva Salve penetrates deep into the skin to ease pain and stiffness, Emma listened with old-fashioned southern Negro gentility—a sweet smile, a soft beam in her eyes, and a gentle nod that confirmed I had her undivided attention.

One summer, Emma accepted the salve I bought for her. I felt certain arther would loosen his grip and planned on hearing that in our next phone call or visit. About four months went by. I traveled back down to D.C.—I worked in New York City at the time—and stopped by Emma's house, but her health and the salve were upstaged by conversations about winter holidays and the food, family, and activities that go with all of that. At the end of the visit, on my way out the door, something happened that sparked a question about arther. I saw the container of Eva Salve on the credenza. I opened it and found the print of a finger on top of the salve as if it had barely been used. I asked Emma about it. "It was all right," she said.

A Culture of Bare Feet and Independence

In this outtake Sebi shows me how culture influences behavior. We're riding to La Ceiba in his mini truck. The tires roll across rough gravel where smooth, tar once lay. Barefooted children walk along the road without a care in the world except getting home or to a makeshift roadside store. Vehicles pass by each child. As if living his own barefoot childhood again, Sebi remarks that it's a scene that hasn't changed in over seventy years in Honduras. We debate why American children lack this kind of freedom. Before we start, Sebi spots a friend's house.

"Oh my gosh," Sebi says.

"What do you want? Something for the man?" Matun asks.

"And you don't have anything with you?" Sebi inquires with haste.

"I have a Green Food."

"A what?"

"I have a Green Food," she repeats, referring to Sebi's product in the portable herbal apothecary she carries in her purse.

"You do?"

"Yeah."

"Okay. Thank you."

"And he probably needs some Chelation. I have that too," she adds.

"That's okay."

"As I was carrying it for Mary."

"Well, that's okay. We'll get another one. She'll get it if he's not there. But I want to see my momma. I want to hear her response because I made that tonic with her in mind."

"What tonic is that Sebi?" I ask. Matun says it's one with iron.

"Plus, plus, plus," Sebi announces, "a bunch of stuff in it. Iron is one. Calcium, magnesium, phosphorous."

"I'll bet your mother is one of the healthiest women on this planet for her age."

A lone toddler tries to pull something from a roadside tree. I wonder what it is. Sebi doesn't know either, but he notices how carefree she wanders around.

"Look how young they are," he says. "They're in the street, in the highway. This is where I was able to cultivate the independence in me that I exhibit. Because look at this little child, he's only about three years of age. He's running in the highway. No one with him. For what? There goes a little girl. See? She's about three too. She's walking with her mommy."

"Yes."

"Understand? On the highway. Look at those little chumps. They're all over the place. They are all over the place. I'm telling you, these boys here they grow up the same way I grew up. That's why when I interrelate with them or I relate to them, I relate to them the way the people related to me when I was a little boy. And it works every time. It works but those things you cannot find in America, because America is of a different culture. It's different. See that little boy?"

"Yes."

"His bare feet? That's the way I was walking, bare feet. No big thing, you know. But in America, 'Bare feet?! My grandson, bare feet!?'"

"No," I say. "In the city you may get that response. But if you were in some southern cities, uh, southern towns, old towns, you would probably see the same thing. I mean they would probably experience the same thing. In the city, in the summertime in New York City, go around any fire hydrant in July and look at what you'll find, right? Harlem, the Bronx."

"I'm talking about every day."

"This is what happens every day?"

"Every day. Everybody walk bare feet. See there?" He points to children walking along the road. I tell him the climate in Honduras allows them to walk bare feet every day. No argument. He agrees.

"That is what I'm saying. The environment provided me with a freedom that my children doesn't exhibit that's born in the United States. My children, my children are stone American in every which way, except for two."

"And are those two Xave—"

"And Sesa."

"Do you want your children to come back down here to live with you when you start your village?" [*silence*] "Uh-oh."

"When you're doing something and you ask people to come in with you, why do you want to do that? If you're building something and those children of yours that want to be a part of it, you don't have to ask them."

"They will come?"

"No stuff," Sebi says.

"They'll be doing it," Matun adds.

"I don't ask them anything. They living their life. And I live mine. I like it here. It's their business if they want to come or if they don't want to come. That's their business. What I care about is my stability, my happiness. I like it here. But because I like it here doesn't mean that they are going to like it here. I have to respect their opinion, right?"

"Yes."

"Okay. It's easy with me."

"Okay, you're happy," I tell him.

"I always was. I always will be until the day I die. It's easy."

"Taking it to the corporate level would be compromising."

"Well, that's not my arena and I don't care about that because those who are in it, they're sick, everyone, everyone sick. They die young. The man that owns Beatrice Food, the cell phone killed him."

"Why do you say that?"

"Because they told him so. He had a tumor on his brain."[4]

"Oh yeah," I recall, "he passed soon after he made that deal. Reginald Lewis is his name."

"And he had billions," Sebi adds. "Me, I don't even have thousands. But I'm happy and I'm seventy-two."

Dis-Ease

The Tree of Forgetfulness: Alive and Well in Darfur
Source: Wole Soyinka, *Of Africa*

A dramatist by profession, I am most partial to rituals. There is, however, one ritual I would rather the world had never known. It has already received mention, and it ranks in my mind as one of the bleakest, most mentally eviscerating rituals that I have ever encountered in decades of exploring the world of dramatic rituals. The ritual took place on the coast of the ancient city of Ouidah, in the present-day Republic of Benin, and its centerpiece was that tree named, for its very function, the Tree of Forgetfulness.

The function was this: when slaves were brought from the inland towns and settlements of West Africa, usually victims of wars and raids engendered for that very purpose, they were placed in stockades, forts, and castle dungeons—the West African coastline is dotted with these—then, before embarkation, subjected to ritual processes which included moving in circles around that infamous tree. The purpose was to make them forget their land, their homes, their kinfolk, and even the very occupations they once knew—in short, forget their former existence, wipe their minds clean of the past and be receptive to the stamp of strange places.

Ease

Chapter 9: Religion Gives Way to Independence
Source: Dr. Sebi, *Sojourn to Honduras Sojourn to Healing*

I grew up in a Garvey house. And growing up in a Garvey house you get this pride, this sense of value that you add to yourself. So I automatically took on that particular persona because my grandmother was one hell of a Black woman. She was uncompromising. She didn't care how big or how small you were. In her eyes you were the same. But she had this sense of value about herself that I seldom see in people. So when I came to America, coming from this house of Garvey, well yes, independence is the thing of the day.

CHAPTER FOUR

On Matters of Identity

Sebi chooses his words carefully. He never uses the words "I think." It's always "I know." He's emphatic about what he knows and doesn't know. He tells it like *he* knows it is. He makes it clear that his Self, his identity, and his life's work stem from that region of the world Europeans named Africa. He tells me, "In the adulteration of my cells, I still remain hooked to that continent from whence I came." And yet, to Sebi, identity runs deeper than geography or ethnicity. What are we then? When I ask him what a human being is, his answer stirs up a debate.

"What is a man?" I ask. "What is a human being?"

"What is a man? I don't even know what a man is," he says.

"No, no, no. When I say man I mean, I'm putting female in that category too. Mankind, a human being. What is it? What are the components of human beings?"

"Well, I don't know any human beings."

"What are you?" I continue. This volley of questions represents new territory for us.

"Wait just a minute. Do you accept the word human being?" he asks me.

"I do, until I come up with something else."

"No, I'm asking you."

"Do I accept it? Yes."

"Okay, good. Well I didn't. I know that I'm not a human being. Because when I was in the forest of Africa, that word didn't exist among us."

"Right." I acknowledge the truth in that statement.

"So whatever it is that we were then, that's what I am now. Before the word 'human being' came into existence, I was something else. And what was that something else? It wasn't important. We were. That's more important than 'I'm a homo sapien. Oh no, I'm a human being. Uh, I'm in a stage of evolutionary process.' Look, hold it. That came straight out of Europe. And I came straight out of Africa. It doesn't apply. Nothing applies. Not that I'm being a rebel. No. I am not being a rebel against anything. I am being. I am someone that is acting in conformity. With the little that I have learned about Africa, and because I was obedient to that, I was able to find a whole lot of other things in the process. So the word 'human'? I don't know what it is. The word homo sapien, oh my God, that's even a long word. I don't even know what that is either."

"But what is that thing?" I ask. "I know you don't like labels. A thing is what it is."

"Why should I like labels? It is a label. But a label really doesn't describe what's inside a bottle."

"Am I in existence? What am I?"

"Hold it. Even the word existence—"

"You said we're African."

"I remember telling you now, that even the word African—"

"Is European," I say.

ON MATTERS OF IDENTITY

"Is not even from the continent. I am today what I was yesterday, a bit adulterated. But in the adulteration, because within the black race, and my own family, my grandmother looked like she just came out of Scotland. So, in the adulteration of my cells, I still remain hooked to that continent from whence I was taken away."

"Ah-h, the continuum," I say, happy to see we were reaching the same plane. "There's a continuum there."

"Well, hold it now. You don't have to tell that to an elephant now. Because an elephant does that just automatically, a gorilla too. So why do you have to put the word continuum or lineage or progression? It was incumbent upon me. That word was never supposed to be said to me either. What happened that I have to be told, 'Oh, you are maintaining the continuum. There's a continuum.' Well, there was a breakage? What was lost in the breakage? You don't want to know that."

"I want to know," I say. That's why I continue with this line of questions. I want him to speak about the components of that continuum, that lineage, that identity.

"No, you don't want to know. You don't even want to know that a black man can cure AIDS. Maybe not you, per se. But the black race doesn't want to know that. Nor anyone else. So, if that was difficult, think about the other stuff I have in my skull."

I quickly learn that if there's one person Sebi claims allegiance to it's himself. Not out of arrogance or conceit, but an adherence to the first law of the universe—self-preservation. That law and self-love are themes that weave their way in and out of our seven-day conversation, with Sebi telling me the absence of both is the root of black America's problems.

"I am doing what any Jew would do for his people," he asserts, "whatever Russian would do for his people, whatever Caucasian, and Chinese, Japanese, or Korean would do for his people. The first law of nature is self-preservation. But when we, the black race, take that position, it's no longer complementing your race, it is being aggressive. It is being other than good. I know that. I've seen it, and I've heard it. Although many times, there have been Blacks who come into the realization of Self, that they become abusive too, with other races, as if we have arrived, so therefore I should offend. No. When you arrive is when you complement. But I come first. My race is first. It has to be first, because it is incumbent upon me by the first law of nature to perpetuate that which I found whole, not to divide it."

"Well, what Adolf Hitler was trying to do, keeping his race pure, was that a good thing?" I ask.

"Who?"

"Adolf Hitler, what he was doing with his scientists, trying to keep his Aryan race pure. Was that a good thing?"

"I have never even read a book that was about Adolf Hitler. And I heard talks about Adolf Hitler, but you ask if Adolf Hitler was right when he tried to preserve the race that he called the Aryan race. I don't know. How would I know if he's right? I know gorillas don't mix with orangutans. It's just naturally, instinctively done. Eagles don't have babies with buzzards. You understand?" he says. "It's like a mule. Whenever a mare gets with a mule, do you know that the mule is never that close like if the mare had a horse baby? Because it's neither a mule nor a horse. No, it's not a horse or a jackass. So who relates to this beast? We are not seeing because it was a Trinidad doctor that showed us that the difference in looking at something and the minute it takes to decipher it, it's different with us, Caucasian, Chinese and everybody else because we are different. We're not better. We just happen to be different. But we always talk about good and bad, better or worse. I don't know where they get those messages from. It takes different fruits to do different things. Okay, which organ is better, the liver or the kidneys? The brain or your toes? You see, they're all made to perform certain functions."

The Nuances of Black Identity

Today, academically, socially, and culturally, black identity and what it means continue to fill books, newspapers, and magazine articles, online and in hard copy. Seldom is the topic absent from TV shows, movies, social media, workshops, and conferences black people attend.

> We are in a post-Black era where the number of ways of being Black is infinite.
> —Touré, *Who's Afraid of Post-Blackness? What It Means to Be Black Now*

> What it means to be Black has grown so staggeringly broad, so unpredictable, so diffuse that blackness itself is indefinable.
> —Casey Hayman, "The Blackness of Blackness," dissertation

> Nothing is wrong with 'African-American' as a racial designation except that the majority of Americans of African descent routinely deny their heritage...We have embraced a concept of beauty that excludes that in which African genes predominate. Toni Morrison's first novel *The Bluest Eye*, captured the essence of black thinking as regards Africa. 'To distance themselves in body, mind, and spirit from all that suggested Africa.'
> —Shannon Sollinger, "The African-American Identity Crisis," *The Washington Post*

Sollinger's statements complement what Sebi tells me when we're in his cabin one afternoon. He says, "One of the things that we overlook, or a few of the things that we overlook among so many, one of them is that we want to tell the world, with our religions, that we love them. We love. We love the world. We love. Oh, it is beautiful to love. I love everybody. But if you take a very close look at that black person that says they love the world, they are wearing lipstick. Their hair is straightened. Their waistline is large, and they are eating acid foods. They are showing us that that which they are saying isn't quite true, because for you to love someone, you must first begin at home. If the love environment is not within you, you cannot love someone else. It is impossible, because the environment isn't there. So, as we tell the Caucasian race that we love them, that is not quite right because we are not exhibiting the love for Self, much less the Caucasian. But if we begin to love ourselves, by cleansing the internal environment, well, naturally the Caucasian is going to see that you're not imitating him anymore. The Caucasian would reap from us that which is uniquely ours. And one of those components is the healing that we bring to the world. Yes, there is love, and we have always felt this way, not only about Caucasians. Black people have no problems with Chinese and Eskimos. So why do we always talk about black and white? We all should love the Caucasian. We all should love Arabs and Chinese and Eskimos because the minute that you entertain hate for someone, you live in that. And you alone live in that. And the African people have taught me a lesson—that an angry heart devours its owner."

Anger aside, Sebi could have equaled Eddie Murphy as a standup comedian, with food and health as topics in his routine. In his cabin one evening, his witty side surfaces when he talks about the Self and what happens when you abandon it.

"Hey, did you know that Self has some great big eyes? And Self always turns against you. But Self always come back and say, 'Hey, I want to remind you, I'm Self. Know who I am? I'm you.' Hey, a woman did a mannequin on Self. She did a job. Oh my God." He laughs. "A mannequin called Self, and got these great big eyes. This woman, what she said was so profound. You got to be very careful with Self. You see, if you don't take care of Self," he says, "that's this woman and this mannequin, and it's true. When you abandon Self, oh, you're in trouble. Kierkegaard, the philosopher, the Danish existentialist, said that the minute you abandon your Self, all you need to do to rectify that, go to a sixteen-story building and just open the window and jump out and splatter yourself on the concrete."[1]

"Wow," I say, listening to him joke. My eyebrows raise with that one, but I could see in his eyes that the wisecracks have stepped aside.

"Yep, Um-hm. That's the solution. Yeah, but it's true, though. When you abandon your Self, what's left? Nothing."[2]

"Yes, that's true. I just believe that this book is going to help people get back to Self."

"Another thing it's going to do," he says, "it's going to remove a lot of fear that the Caucasian have in us, with us, about us."

Humble, Frank, with a Tinge of Vulgarity

Back on the road in the mini truck one morning, Sebi, Matun, and I pass an intersection where chaos blankets the sky. A mass of birds circles and cackles so loud they drown out the traffic below. I record the ambience of this flock that Matun calls nigga birds. Sebi drives pass the spectacle. A few blocks down the road he pulls up alongside a friend. He speaks to him in Spanish, and gives him some herbal compounds for his eyes.

It's the kind of generosity I witness several times that week. But, like clockwork, Sebi shrugs off all recognition of his acts of kindness. Even when we talk about his family's achievements, like his nephew who decided to buy an airline, to Sebi, it's no big deal.

"Well that's nothing," he says one evening back at his cabin. "That's fantastic."

"Naw," he says, in the consistently demure tone he uses when a compliment is given.

"Buying an airline Sebi? I mean, come on. It's not like going to the store to buy some chewing gum. That's great."

"Well, when the man came and told me he was cured of AIDS I wasn't excited, and I wasn't surprised, and I wasn't like, 'Wow! I cure AIDS, fellas!' I told the man thank you and went about my business. It's as simple as that, no big thing."

"You're very humble."

"No, but hey, what is humility? What is non-humility? You know, hey, you have to do something, you do it."

"So all this wisdom comes from the vibration, the divine order, your wanting to live better and be healed."

"I didn't want anything. I didn't want anything. It came. And then I said I was going to do something that would upset the balance of things, and I did it. But out of that came healing, and I didn't expect that, because I didn't want to be a healer, like I said. I didn't want to be a healer. Because in America, to be a healer you have to walk a certain way, and you have to talk a certain way," he croons. "You even have to move your hands a certain way. You have to fold, and you have to walk with grace. And then all of that makes up that persona that's going to heal people. But the end product is never forthcoming."

"The end product is never forthcoming?"

ON MATTERS OF IDENTITY

"The end product was never forthcoming from those who call themselves all of that. With me, I'm loud. I'm undisciplined."

"I want you to talk about that," I request. It's an appeal for clarification. "Because there's a section in the book where you say, 'I'm a vulgar person. Sometimes I stand between me and my own representation because people always ask Why don't you appear on this show? or Why don't you appear on that show, like *Oprah*?' And then you say you're a vulgar person. And I want you to address that. Why do you feel you're a vulgar person and an undisciplined person considering all that you've done, all the healing, all the good things that you've done?" There's silence for about thirty seconds. "Address that."

"The church said it," he answers.

"The church said you're vulgar?"

"In Memphis."

"The church in Memphis?"

"They say I cursed," he recounts. "That's what they said, that I cursed."

"You used profanity."

"That's being vulgar."

"You're just repeating what they said," I confirm.

"Yeah."

I refer to his memoir, *The Cure*. "No, but in this section of the book you say yourself you're vulgar. You stand in the way of your—"

"Well," he jumps in, "I'm a whole lot of things, according to those people. But I don't mind that. It doesn't matter. What matters is I am what I am. And if what I am I like, I like that." He chuckles.

I'm taken off-guard when Sebi tells this story about church people who criticized him for cursing, and even more surprised when he agrees with them. Vulgar and undisciplined? He's satisfied to end the story there but I press him for a deeper explanation—and not for journalistic reasons. I refuse to store impressions of a vulgar yet successful healer in my mind.

"Yeah, but do you really think you're vulgar and undisciplined?"

"I do think that I am undisciplined. I don't think that either. I know that."

"Describe 'undisciplined.' What have you done or haven't done that makes you believe that you're undisciplined?" I ask.

"I don't believe that. I know that. I never use the word 'believe' in my vocabulary," he reminds me.

"How are you undisciplined?"

"Because I would do anything at any time, things that you would least suspect. Disciplined people don't do that. And disciplined people went through a particular curricular and ethical training. With me, I didn't have any of that. I would do anything at any time, things that you would least suspect."

"Well, the things that you do turn out okay. Have you ever been so spontaneous and undisciplined that the thing you've done turned out wrong or turned out badly?"

"I don't do bad things. I'm saying I would do things that would shock you. But a disciplined person would never do that, like for instance, I'm on a train," he recalls, "and a woman said, 'You're a baby.' I said, 'Of course I am. I'm hungry and I'm nursing. Feed me.'"

I chuckle at that one. Sebi was a serious healer with razor-sharp, uncompromising opinions, but he had a playful sense of humor that balanced it all.

"You see," he continues, "a disciplined person would never take it to that level. But I would."

ON MATTERS OF IDENTITY

"Right. You sound like a very—," I pause, fishing for the right word, "it's not like you're undisciplined. You don't sound undisciplined. You sound like a very blunt—"

"Blunt?"

"Blunt person."

"Where's that blunt from?" he quips. We laugh. "Where do you get that blunt from?"

"Frank and very blunt person. That's what it sounds like you are."

"What do I know about blunt and all of that, girl?"

"I wouldn't say undisciplined Sebi." There's some subconscious thing going on with me that refuses to accept negative criticism from Sebi or about Sebi. Two or three times a year, I search the internet for defamatory or "quack" comments about him. When I find one, I'm usually Johnny-on-the-spot to defend his African Bio Mineral Balance system. I suppose that's the trait of a protégé or disciple, which I have been since my research corroborated practically everything Sebi has said about the food and health connection. He may have been slightly off base when he talked about the carrot—it is a natural plant; only the orange carrot, a hybrid, is man-made—but all in all, Sebi was on point with the information he shared.

"Yes," he continues. "I am undisciplined because I said people that are disciplined, they have to do things such as go to the sorority meeting. They have to go to church. They have to go to a job that they have to do things a certain way. And they have to behave a certain way in a certain circumstance, when I do not afford myself those environments because I already know that I may take my penis out to go and piss in front of somebody if I need to piss. And they are not going to appreciate that."

"That makes you undisciplined?"

"Well, that's what the folks said. That's vulgar and undisciplined. But when I live in the forest, I can take my dick out and piss anywhere I want to piss. But I can't do it now because they put concrete on the ground, and now it is prohibited to piss on the concrete. I gotta piss in a machine they call a toilet."

By the end of my week in Honduras, I'd grown accustomed to Sebi's barefaced responses. Pearls of wisdom usually followed. That's Sebi.

Dis-Ease

Malnutrition: A major cause of death in children
Source: UNICEF for every child, West and Central Africa

Six million children are affected by life-threatening severe acute malnutrition in West and Central Africa. Multiple factors including land and crop degradation, periodic droughts and weather-related shocks, poverty, limited access to basic food staples and essential services, and population growth, contribute to emergency levels of malnutrition in the region.

Malnutrition is not only about lack of food; a combination of other causes lead to malnutrition in children, including: diet at home, illnesses such as malaria and water-borne diseases, limited access to clean water and sanitation infrastructure, and knowledge about safe hygiene practices, lack of access to health services, and inadequate child feeding practices.

Ease

Chapter 7: Food and the African Gene
Source: Dr. Sebi, *Sojourn to Honduras Sojourn to Healing*

Well, the food that we eat is the very substance that causes the whole hormonal structure of the body to go haywire because it's of an acid base. So you're going to get acid thoughts. I listened to the guru. Well, I was not encouraged to any great extent because I know that words do not put you in a cosmic balance. It is the food that you eat that would reconnect you with energies of life and then words are unnecessary because you could see. You're connected. Like the eagle. How come the eagle could make that nest? How could the beaver make the dam? The spider makes his web? Because it is coded. But you have to be cleansed of the poisons that you were unaware were entering your brain.

CHAPTER FIVE

On Matters of Food and Health

Monday morning, I leave my cabin and head over to see Sebi. I walk across the two-foot wide, streaming canal that runs through the middle of the Usha Village cabins—seven on each side of the canal, painted in different pastels: pink, yellow, or lime green. When I open the wooden screened door of Sebi's cabin, I grin and watch a surprising scene: Dr. Sebi—curer of diabetes, high blood pressure, and cancer; herbalist to celebrities; advocate of alkaline food—eating cookies with Matun. I sit down and join them. Every now and then Sebi falls off the wagon. I couldn't help thinking that the renowned healer was cheating on his die-hard alkaline diet. Sebi sees it another way.

"We call it cheating instead of a conditioning," he says. "It's not a cheating. That doesn't exist, because the gorilla never cheats. The gorilla eats exactly what he was designed to eat throughout his lifetime.[1] So why is it that the gorilla, when he finds himself in a zoo, he too begins to cheat? Because they feed him bananas. Gorilla does not eat bananas in the forest.² But in a zoo he eats bananas. When we were in the forest, we didn't eat rice and beans. Goats and cows, that represent poison, because there isn't any nutritionist or biochemist that could show scientifically the benefits of animal blood in the human body. Blood represents disease. Blood is the carrier of disease. And the liver is the filter. So how could ingesting the blood of an animal be useful in my nutrition? So cheating is a conditioning. It's not a conscious, deliberate act."

"What we're doing now, we're eating cookies," I say, chewing what tastes like a gingersnap.

"Well, we are what you would call cheating."

"We are cheating then?"

"No, but remember, we are only submitting to that part of us that has been so conditioned throughout the years," he clarifies. "We didn't have sugar in Africa because we didn't grow cane. We didn't have wheat in Africa because to eat wheat in Africa, we must have had a laboratory to create wheat because wheat is a laboratory product.³ There again, we lived exactly the way the Creator wanted us to live."

"Today there is fast food," I say. "With the availability of fast food people are bigger now. Do you think things that have gone wrong with people in that area and throughout the United States is because of diet?"

"Well, we would have to attribute it to diet, because I have thirty-one years of experience. When I remove the diet from people, not only is that physical change seen, but other changes. Like, for instance, here we have Mr. Martinez from Descombros. Descombros, Honduras, which is not too far from here. *Descombros* means 'the decline.' That's where the trains are going to the east and the decline, at some point, going downhill. This man came to me with high blood pressure, diabetes, and impotence. At the ending of six weeks' treatment, the man came in my office with a gun."

"I remember that story."

"You see, so the man showed not only was the diabetes and impotence reversed, but that he didn't need the gun anymore. And I have had many of those examples shown to me, where the individual goes into a state that is so relaxed that he is not threatened by anything or anyone because our greatest enemy is ourselves."

Sebi talks about food and his point of view while he relaxes, with his T-shirt-clad chest upright and resting on his pillows. Gone are the tension and defenses that topics like leaders and philosophy bring. He tells me a story about love and marriage and how food has an uncanny way of affecting them. He mentions a Honduran man who had diseases that interfered with his marriage—diabetes and high blood pressure. The man was a ball of rage until Sebi used herbs and changed the man's diet to improve his situation.

"We have to go back to the food of our fathers and of our mothers if we are to visit the peaceful zone again in life, like we once exhibited in Africa. No longer do we have that peace. We show it in our marriage. I see it in marriage. I see it right in Aruba with C. C. Charles. When he was at odds with his wife, he didn't speak to her for sixteen years. What was causing that? The food that he was eating. But after he changed his diet, he told me to go tell his wife that he loved her. But what happened? I'm not a psychiatrist. I'm not a neuropathologist. But I changed his mental environment by changing the electrochemical structure of his body. And there he is now, loving his wife, took her on a vacation. And that is the way it is. Love begins at home."

Cassava's Hidden Nature

After thirty years of lectures, interviews, and consultations with his clients, Sebi knew, without a shadow of a doubt, that food was a touchy subject with people. When he told audiences that food, for generations, has stimulated taste buds and filled bellies but offered no nourishment or strength for the immune system, eyebrows raised, and sighs spread through the hall. Yet he plowed through because he wanted us to know what he knew so that better nutritional decisions could be made. We'd have more options. Sebi often said the only option some people reach for now is acid food.

We ride through La Ceiba one day. Acidic food like cassava comes up. He says, "The amount of glucose in the cassava is going to stimulate you, and you're going to feel good. So there's every reason that justify eating cassava.[4] But then, what the person was unaware of is that the cassava is going to stimulate him until age forty-five, and then the cassava is going to collect. The cassava is going to collect from you what it is doing, what it is designed to do. Cassava was designed to harden your arteries and to send the blood sugar out of whack."[5]

Cassava is a cyanide-laced tuberous plant.[6] Many "foods" are made with it. Tapioca is one. Gari, a staple of Nigerian cuisine, is another.

"But they say," Sebi continues, "they also told Africa that they can drink cow milk. They say that black people needed A, B, C and 1, 2, 3. They say, but they forgot that Africa existed millions of years before there was an A, B, C. Yeah. Yeah," he sings.

Alkaline Food—A Nourisher

The benefits of an alkaline diet are not debated, but Sebi tells me that eating healthy is a real struggle for his clients. And in the past, for him too. He knows that food customs, when left unchecked, wreak havoc on people around the world. "Hey, Nigerians, you can't eat gari," he shouts.

"Well, that's really interesting what you said about food and peace and what happens to the brain when you remove the food that blocks it," I say.

"You see, that's common sense. If you eat acid food, you would definitely entertain acid thoughts, because your body is stressed. It has contracted. Acid food contracts the central nerve system. Alkaline food relaxes the central nerve system.[7] I'm chillin'. Many of us pursue it by ingesting stimulants. Well, a stimulant will let you down and put you in a greater deficit. But a nourisher—oh, that complements from the minute you put it into your mouth."

Matun echoes Sebi's recommendations. One afternoon she rides with Sebi and me to a rental car company. When Sebi goes inside to check on a car, Matun and I continue a conversation about the best way to eat. It's not rocket science or a cross-country marathon. It's a commitment to health Matun insists.

"If you refrain three days, only three days, and you do not put something in your mouth that was created by a man, and you utilize anything that was created by our Creator or Creation, you would get some cosmic connection. It's not a message. It's a deliverance."

"Yes, that's the word I'm looking for," I say.

"Deliverance," she repeats.

"Now we're on the same plane."

"And you cannot deliver yourself unless you stop putting dead things in your mouth."

CHAPTER SIX

Cosmic Arrangement of Life

The cosmos—limitless, vast. The cosmic arrangement of life is a major topic in our conversations. Sebi tells me that whatever nature puts in place for him to do, he does it, including healing and building Usha Village. No academic degree. No formal schooling. His school is the sea and the world and whatever nature propels him to do within them. One morning in his cabin, Sebi tells me how Americans live labels rather than the cosmic arrangement of life.

"What is the cosmic arrangement?" I ask.

"It's an energy that you receive."

Matun joins the conversation. "So you're saying it's an expression of life?"

"Well, it is an expression but on what level to be understood?" he says. "You feel that. It's a vibration, because see, where did I get the idea to go and put the stuff on the lady's head? You see, it's a vibration. A vibration that we don't trust. But I trust it. I trust it because it is coming from me, not from Socrates or Plato."

"So you feel that because we don't trust it—" I say.

"Ah, ha! You're never rewarded by it. That's correct. If you trust it, you will see the beauty in it. But sometimes we are forced and compelled to go against it because the industry tells you you have to. Like many industries told our sisters, 'You better straighten your hair.'"

"It's what? You better straighten—"

He laughs and continues. "You better straighten your hair or else you're not going to get this job. Now, look at an industry who compels a woman to deny God to get a job. Oh no. Oh no. These are just superficial things that we see every day. That's why I can see the hermit, not the hermit, the monk. I can see why the monk separates from society, because he could see the fallacy. He could see the inconsistency. So he knows that he cannot change it. So he just separates himself and say I'm going to enjoy me. And that's what I'm doing. I'm going to enjoy me because I know that I cannot change the condition of things as they are right now. It would be impossible. I don't even dream to do that. I would like to make them better, because I see the violence that is being precipitated because of the food that we eat. But the food industry is now going to get on Dr. Sebi's neck. But I'm not Oprah Winfrey.[1] When they jump on her neck, she didn't have an answer for them.[2] Well, I would like for them to jump on my neck, like the FDA and the judicial system when they jump on me in New York. See, I like to be jumped on because I need to be jumped on. Why? Because the American, the Caribbean, or the African people even, doesn't have the faintest of an idea of the components that support the life of the African people whether in America or in Africa, the Caribbean."

Sebi intended to fill that void. He created Usha Research Institute and his African Bio Mineral Balance system to teach a deeper awareness of health and nutrition. He dismissed the label African American, leaving me to wonder why it isn't the best description of a people who have adapted two cultures.

"Instead of saying I'm an African born in America, I'm saying an African American. When did we become a hybrid in the transition? When did we become a hybrid?" he asks. "An African American is a hybrid. An American is an American and an African is an African. When did we become African American? That's impossible. Those are the things that hurt us. Those are the things that we support. We support these things. But when we say we are an African, then we have to put in motion those components that belong to the culture of the African. As an African American, I have no culture. There is no culture. There is no such thing as a history of African American. But there is a history of Africans."

I tell him okay. I understand his point but, a statement comes to my mind, one that surfaces many times in conversations about black identity: "We're not a monolithic people." I hear it every now and then in media interviews or read it in black publications and on social media. I gather from Sebi that's the problem, that straying from the core or as he puts it, the African resonance.

"Not of African American," he continues, "and this is why being a hybrid, we're going to always think in a hybrid way."

Sebi's mini truck rolls along on a smooth paved road on the outskirts of La Ceiba, where mountains of thick brush surround us, including ceiba trees, also known as kapok trees according to Frommer's guide. Needless to say, medicinal plants are plentiful in Central America. Indigenous people, especially older ones, know them well. Garifunas—Afro-Honduran people in Belize, Guatemala, and Honduras—know over three hundred medicinal plants that heal. But that knowledge of nature is waning in young children and young adults.[3]

Sebi sees a man on the street who reminds him of a friend. "Boy, he look like Grafton with his hat down like that. Isn't that something?"

Matun agrees.

"Oh Grafton, I love you. He's gone boy, four years ago. Yeah, my friend Grafton. Yeah, yes, yes, yes. My wife here told me that, or she made me aware of something I was totally unaware of. She told me that I have been talking about things such as food. If it isn't godly, it isn't good. Like the sister who wrote the tune in Philadelphia, 'If nature didn't make it, don't take it. If nature didn't make it, don't take it. Don't take it if nature didn't make it.' So I was totally unaware that that applies to everything that is in existence. And she said to me one day,

'And what about a dog?'

I said, 'What about a dog?'

She said, 'Well, dog isn't made by God so there must be something about this beast.'

"Come to find out a dog and a cat have over three hundred germs that is only indicative to them.[4] That is because they are not germs. What are they? They are nature's police.[5] Natural animal doesn't have those things. You don't need to take a natural animal to a vet. You need to take a pet to a vet. God didn't make dogs. See, those are the realities that healing brings, that it is difficult for people to give up the conditioning. It is difficult, sister. I know it is difficult. Sebi knows, because the one thing that Sebi couldn't give up for a long time was beans and rice, and even now I eat it once in a while, knowing that the stuff is bad. Yeah, that's reality, okay?"

"Okay," I repeat.

"You see, that's why I said when you begin to talk about truth, how many of us, including Sebi, are prepared for it?"

CHAPTER SEVEN

Usha Village 2008—
Dr. Sebi, His Guests,
and Dembali

It's September 2008 when Sebi and I arrive in Honduras to work on Dembali, a book he decided to usher ahead of his autobiography. He insisted it has a more urgent message than his life's story: When something of value is given to people, why do they reject it, and how do they overcome the rejection?

The two-week trip begins in Roatán, a Honduran island about a thirty-minute boat ride from the mainland. It's home to the world's second-largest barrier reef, the Mesoamerican system—at that time a snorkeler's playground bursting with vibrant pastel and fluorescent coral and tropical fish. Today, global warming, pollution, and the red lionfish invasion have changed all of that. They affect the region so much that the reef is now an endangered ecosystem.

We stay at the east end of Roatán, at a remote resort called Paya Bay. Smaller than the luxury hotels on the island, Paya Bay sits on a coastal bluff that overlooks the sun-splashed Caribbean Sea. It boasts two beaches, including one for guests who practice naturism, commonly known as nudists.

Instead of a boat ride, we reach this oasis by twin-engine plane from La Ceiba in late morning, but something is amiss at the airport. The clerk at the customs counter informs us that my luggage, filled with clothes and recording equipment, didn't reach the island. I glance at Sebi for reassurance that this is not a problem, but instead he gives me an aloof smile and look, as if it's just one of those things that happens in Honduras. No big deal. I'm stunned by Sebi's indifference, so much so that the clerk telling me there'll be a search for my luggage is a muffle in my ears. He's not coming through. My body stilled, all I can see in my mind's eye are my toiletries, night clothes, cameras and recorders stranded somewhere in the world, lost forever. Things are replaceable, but to me there's a value beyond dollars on each item in the suitcase.

Paya Bay's driver arrives at the airport to pick us up. He's a stout, sixtyish Central American man with trimmed, moderately gray hair. I walk slightly behind Sebi to the waiting car. I'm at wit's end now as I extend a listless hello to the driver and sit in the back seat behind Sebi. I gaze out the window, backtracking my steps from the Los Angeles terminal to the customs counter in Honduras. Sebi, on the other hand, is having a cheerful conversation in Spanish with the driver.

What snaps me back to the present is the ride along Roatán's countryside. A cow with a couple of bulging ribs grazes on the edge of a rough dirt road. Houses attached to wooden slats sit about five feet aboveground. Flood control, I think. A woman looks out the window of one of them. Sebi waves to her as the car passes by. She's a cousin, Sebi tells me. Sharing this information restores some camaraderie between us, but he's still obviously unfazed about the missing luggage. The driver then tells Sebi in Spanish that he'll go back to the airport later to get it. Sebi translates the message, relieving me to a point.

Just as I'm about to retreat to that faraway place where wandering luggage goes, the driver pulls up to a grassy open lot near a walkway to a cluster of cottages built on a cliff. The panoramic view in the car's windshield pulls me up from my slump. It's as if the Caribbean Sea, visible from the driver's side all the way to the passenger's side, coaxes me to step from the hood of the car and tiptoe across the famously turquoise water inches away. I accept the invitation later on in the evening when I trek down to sea level to get a closer look at the water. By week's end I've dipped my entire body in, but not before my luggage arrives. When it reaches Paya Bay and I'm ready to shoot pictures, the trip's already in a bit of a tailspin.

The night before the driver dropped off the luggage, Sebi offered me his dental cream to clean my teeth and his pajama top for me to sleep in. But the beach's euphoric pull on me had long disappeared. I was restless again. I pass on Sebi's offer.

He leaves Paya Bay and me for a whole day, shortly after the driver delivers the retrieved luggage, which Sebi suspected the baggage handlers deemed too heavy to put on the small commuter plane filled with passengers and lighter suitcases.

I explore the resort alone, my cameras in tow. I walk down a trail lined with dense flora and palm trees that leads to the smaller of the two beaches, the nudist beach. Wide-eyed, I watch lizards scamper in front of me while small iguanas stroll by in the bushes along the trail's edge. I shoot still and moving pictures and spend a few minutes talking with other Paya Bay guests, including a nude tour guide. Sebi couldn't have chosen a more appropriate location to talk about dembali. There's a sense of ease here, that carefree, uninhibited energy he raves about.

When he returns to Paya Bay, I'm ready to return to the feelings I had before my luggage went missing. I'm ready to work on dembali and shoot photos of Sebi. But Sebi has other plans. He's still lukewarm but ready to show me the island and his family. The SUV he brings back to Paya Bay is the vehicle he uses. It takes us from Paya Bay to West End, Roatán, from a small waterfront community lined with shotgun houseboats and cabins to the home of Ploney Jones, the boat captain that gave a young Alfredo Bowman his first merchant seaman job back in the 1950s. We arrive at an east-end dock where a young Afro-Honduran man who appears to be in his late twenties and a small motor boat wait to take us to a thirty-acre community around the island's bend. No paved roads exist on that part of the island, making it necessary to commute by boat. Sebi's cousins, ages seven to sixty, own and live on the coastal property. It stands out as a perfect example of the independent "village" living Sebi encourages. Makeshift but functional accommodations serve the family villagers: a mail service shed, a boat dock supplied with gasoline, a three-table dining room and store counter, and a large outdoor supply cabinet that stores nonperishable food and household goods.

USHA VILLAGE 2008—DR. SEBI, HIS GUESTS, AND DEMBALI

A half dozen cottages are scattered across the land, each one a stone's throw from the Caribbean Sea. Palm trees and other tropical plants hover high and low above them. A few plastic water bottles and soda cans peep from underneath sand and blades of grass, while a brown pet cow, with her legs buckled under her body, lounges in a cottage's front yard. A small island that Sebi inherited from his grandfather juts out across the sea from his relatives' community. It's an all-day visit, with me snapping pictures most of the time: Sebi and his cousins rock climbing, boats big and small, and a young man built like a defensive linebacker who steers them.

When it's time for us to leave Roatán and head over to La Ceiba, then on to Sebi's healing center Usha, we travel by a double-decker ferry with outdoor seats on the top deck near the engine. Most passengers sit indoors on the lower level. Sebi decides we should sit outdoors. I'm certain this on-deck, near-the-engine ride sparks memories for him. In his merchant seaman days, he loaded and unloaded cargo and worked in the ship's engine room. But on this commuter boat, gas fumes stream out and up to the top deck. I suggest we move to seats indoors but Sebi feels the smell is tolerable. It's okay, he says, but I go inside anyway. He stays and talks with other passengers, mostly Mesoamerican descendants and a few black Hondurans.

When we arrive at Usha, Sebi settles down and lounges in his cabin, where he meets and greets people who have come to see his village. Two days later, he decides to hold an impromptu lecture for all of his guests who are visiting that week: men and women from Jamaica, the UK, the US, and Honduras. All eight of them are black with natural hairstyles, including a man and woman with locs (reggae singer Junior Lion and his publicist). They range in ages from twenty to fifty-five and wear clothes essential for moving around a tropical rainforest: sun dresses, T-shirts, cotton shorts, dashikis, and sleeveless tank tops. Some journeyed to Sebi's healing center for health reasons, others for sightseeing and relaxation. It's a first-time visit for all of them.

The lecture begins one humid, 80-degree morning in the circular dining room, after guests have eaten a breakfast of fruit, vegetable salad, and straight, no-chaser liquid herbs (the bitters). Wood tables and high-back chairs are placed alongside the dining room's windows. I set up a video recorder and cassette recorder.

Soon after he enters the pastel-yellow dining room he built, Sebi's persona shifts from friend to respected teacher about to unleash another experience-backed lesson from his brain. There's one other high-back chair in the middle of the room that faces the diners. He strides over to it and focuses. His eyes steer clear of mine. I assume he's still lukewarm about the boat ride. He sits and observes the faces of the semi-circle of guests as if he's trying to determine if they can handle the truth he's about to reveal in the way he's going to reveal it. His assessment ends. Dembali begins.

He begins with a story about his grandmother, Mama Hay. It shines light on a way of raising children in Central America that Sebi feels may be viewed in a negative way in the United States.

"When I was sixteen years of age, I was working here in Honduras because, you know, I had to take care of my grandmother. To show you something where societies and cultures change, I lived with my grandmother from age eight until twenty. If my grandmother was in the United States and she had done with me in the United States what she did with me, she would have gone to jail. What would she have gone to jail for? Child abuse. Because I was thirteen years of age when I had to pay the rent. I had to buy my grandmother clothes. But my grandmother was cooking for me, you understand? My grandmother cooked for me. And I would work. I paid the rent, which was only two and half dollars a month. I would go to work and come back, go to work and come back home, go to work and come back home. Me and my grandmother. But like I said, if my grandmother was in the United States, governed by a philosophy, my grandmother would have been in jail and I would have never reaped from my grandmother what I got from her. Because at thirteen is when you just begin to go to school, right? Am I right? You learn in school. But no, instead I listened to this black woman. And it was ba-a-d. I gained a lot from her, by being with her all day long."

"People emphasize the trust, the assistance, and the solidarity that kin owe to one another," says a 1995 U.S. Library of Congress book by Tim Merrill titled *Honduras: A Country Study*.[1] The book's research illustrates the respect for family and culture Sebi and other Hondurans have. On page 90 Merrill states, "Family loyalty is an ingrained and unquestioned virtue; from early childhood, individuals learn that relatives are to be trusted and relied on, whereas those outside the family are implicitly at least, suspect. In all areas of life and at every level of society, a person looks to family and kin for both social identity and assistance."

By now you know that Sebi is the father of several children, approximately twenty of them ranging in ages from six to sixty-four at the time of this writing. He's candid about this information—in public lectures and private conversations. He shares it freely, the same way he shares stories about the impotence he experienced as a young man. Like I said in the introduction, Sebi was an open book. And yet there's healing in his frankness.

"You know," he says to his audience, "this village was developed by two people. It was my wife and Matun. My wife left. My wife divorced me seven years before I even know she was divorced from me, which I didn't feel that that was bad. After many years, remember what we said, the central nerve system has been damaged. I was married to my wife for many, many years. I live in my world. And I wasn't going to compromise my world for my wife or for nobody. I can't, even if I wanted to because I don't know how to do that. I could only be Sebi. She, on the other hand, she had to live the same way. I didn't want to divorce the woman, but what I did, I began to make babies with other women and have other wives. I had three wives at one point."

Before we continue with Sebi's lecture in the dining room at Usha, I present background information about "fathering" and marriage the Honduran way, again from *Honduras: A Country Study*:

> In Honduras, there are three accepted forms of marriage: civil, religious, and free unions. Both serial monogamy and polygamous unions are socially accepted. Annulment is difficult to obtain through the Roman Catholic Church; this fact, in addition to the expense involved, makes couples reluctant to undertake a religious marriage. Civil marriage is relatively common.
>
> No shame accrues to the man who fathers many children and maintains several women as mistresses. Public disapproval follows only if the man fails to assume the role of "head of the family" and to support his children.

"If the resonance was there," Sebi continues, "what you call affinity, chemical affinity, when chemical affinity is there, none of you, either male or female, would be dissatisfied with the other.

USHA VILLAGE 2008—DR. SEBI, HIS GUESTS, AND DEMBALI

But when you come together based on something artificial, the day would come that affinity is going to drive you guys apart. And why? The central nerve system has been damaged. When the man and woman first met, there were flowers and 'Baby, I love you,' and long conversations on the phone and listening to each other. But when they get married, and thirty-five years go by, 'Paul, would you please tell your daddy to turn the television down?' He's sitting right there, but she's going to tell her son to tell the father. How did that occur? Ah-h, they continue to eat those starches, that blood and that is taking a toll now because it's cumulative. It's taken a toll now because both of them have increased in quantity starch and blood. So naturally, when the man and woman first met in their early twenties or late twenties, they're not as polluted as you would be in your fifties, right? You've got thirty years of accumulation of starch and blood. 'He always...' But didn't you see that when you first met him? No, you didn't. No, you didn't because you both were eating the foods that bring that anger out now. You're going to begin to say things that you didn't say before. That is what happened to my marriage.

"I love my wife. I love my wife very much. I love her now. I love her. I guess I love her more now than ever. She divorced me seven years before me even knowing, before I even knew. Um-hm. She thought that maybe doing that that way, it would relieve pain on both sides, right? It's as simple as that because a woman—a woman more than males—she could recognize when the time has come to leave. I wasn't going to divorce her because I have a beautiful son with her. Oh yes, I wasn't going to do that. But she, in her frustration, she did it. She had to. Now what am I leading to? The adulterated sperm. You see why we sick? All of us in here are sick.

"Do you think that our great-grandmothers, my great-great-grandmother only ate herbs and fruits, and my grandmother, and my momma and my daddy? When I was born, do you think that I would have been born with asthma? I was born with asthma. How could a baby be born into the world with a disease? Because it came out of a diseased body. And name it now. I want one of you in this room to tell me which one of us came out of a mother that was clean? Nobody. Nobody. We are a product of a sick mother and father. So when we find ourselves not able to decipher when we have been given a situation, you know, a situation in life, we get frustrated. 'Why me? Why me?' Just go back and take inventory. Just go back to your momma and your daddy, and they momma and they daddy, daddy, daddy, daddy, daddy. We were born compromised. So now, when you come here, you're getting degrees of the journey back."

When he's done revealing how the effects of dembali influenced behavior in his own family, Sebi jumps right into talks of the central nervous system and his research in Russia.

"Day before yesterday, we talked about foods and what we're doing wrong, but today we're going to talk about what causes us to behave the way we behave. What is the system that they made sure they affected and they destroyed in us? Our central nerve system. And I want for each and every one of you, when you leave from here, you're going to have the opportunity to try to see how we have been affected. Now, I went to Russia in 1970. I went there because I want to do research on herbs because I heard that Russians had taken a dog's head and grafted it on another dog, on one dog. The dog had two heads.[2] I said what? They sure did.

"So now, what did I see? There was a man in Russia that very few people know about. Ivan Petrovich Pavlov. You know about him? Conditional reflexes. Conditioning reflexes. The Russian was experimenting. Because they were going to send into the world a group of people that had no feelings for themselves but

USHA VILLAGE 2008—DR. SEBI, HIS GUESTS, AND DEMBALI

for the state. They didn't want you thinking for yourself. You had to think in favor of the state. So to accomplish that they knew that there had to be a system in the body that they would control, and that is your central nerve system. So, what did they do? They used a dog.[3]

"The Pavlovian dog is a dog that does things against his own existence. That's us. That's us. Pavlov took this dog and conditioned that dog to drink a bowl of milk at a certain hour—eleven o'clock. The dog would come and drink the milk. Go back to your cage dog. They would ring a bell after a while. When the dog hear the bell, he knew it was eleven o'clock. What do you mean it was a clock? Dog doesn't know about clock, right? But he heard the bell. So, he would come out and drink the milk and he would go back. He heard the bell. But one day, they didn't ring the bell. And the dog was there at eleven o'clock. Isn't that us?"

Dembali's reasons why we do what we do—why and how we reject the beneficial in matters of race, health, family, and culture—are front and center in Sebi's lecture. Centuries-old conditioning tops his list for the reasons why.

"I could take this fruit here. Very, very, very, very few people in the world know what this fruit is. I brought students from the university in the United States, and I sat them down and I put an apple and one of these. I said, 'Which fruit would you eat?' They took the apple. They had to. Everybody took the apple. Why? They didn't know this. This is *icacos*.[4] The apple was made. Not this. But that's all they knew, like the Pavlovian dog. That's all they knew. But the apple has what? Lead. Inorganic lead. They couldn't use this. This has potassium iodide in it. This thing grows in the ocean, in sand. But they didn't know anything about it. This fruit would nourish you. But when you're conditioned, you can't see it. So, what I did, I had a bowl.

I said, 'Now eat.' They say, 'Who? What's that?' I said, 'You see, I'm your brother. I bring you something to eat, but when the man put an apple in front of you, you grabbed it, and you ate it thinking it was good. But I'm your brother, but you're thinking if I'm going to poison you.' That is what they did to us."

Sebi holds out his hand to show how steady it is. "Now, when I was sixteen, I couldn't do this. I used to wonder why I was nervous, nervous, nervous. Haven't you all seen youngsters that were nervous, nervous, nervous? You never knew why? Now, what did they put in the milk to condition the dog? Sugar. Sugar is one of the most dangerous drugs that you could ever use. You ask my little daughter. My little daughter has an aunt. She has two little boys. My little daughter's mother's name is Fannie. The little boy didn't like for his mother to prepare his bottle. Fannie used to prepare the little boy bottle. And the little boy could never take the bottle from his mother. It would be raining, and the little boy want his mother to go outside across the street to get Fannie to fix the bottle. What was in the bottle that Fannie was putting in there? Sugar. The momma didn't know. The mother had to get Fannie because the momma didn't give the child sugar. Sugar was considered a drug, a very bad drug up until the eighteenth century."

It's still considered a drug. In 2013 Healthline.com wrote,

A highly cited study in the journal *Neuroscience & Biobehavioral Reviews* found that sugar—as pervasive as it is—meets the criteria for a substance of abuse and may be addictive to those who binge on it. It does this by affecting the chemistry of the limbic system, the part of the brain that's associated with emotional control. The study found that 'intermittent access to sugar can lead to behavioral and neurochemical changes that resemble the effects of a substance of abuse.' It's these findings that spurred Paul van der Velpen, head of Amsterdam's health services, to warn people that sugar is a drug, 'just like alcohol and tobacco.'"

"Sugar is a drug," Sebi continues. "Why should it be? But when you ask the conditioned student and person,

'Well, it came from the cane.'

Well, so?

'Well, cane is natural.'

How do you know that? Just how do you know that cane is natural? Who told you that? Because remember, everything we know or think that we know, we got it out of a book and from the mouth of a schoolteacher. But the schoolteacher and the book didn't talk about icacos. Because the teacher himself didn't know. This happened to my daughter in Los Angeles.

"My daughter's name is Xave. Xave was home with us until she was sixteen. And she sick and tired of being with Dad and Mom alone. She want friends now. The girl is sixteen now, right? Xave used to sleep on the floor with us. Didn't have no Christmas clothes. Didn't have no Christmas shoes. We had a big room on Washington Boulevard in L.A. We didn't have much money. She would sleep on the floor over there, and her momma and I would sleep over here—on the floor. But that little girl never complained once to us about Christmas and Christmas clothes. A woman came one day, on Christmas Eve and said,

'Xave, I know Daddy gonna buy you some Christmas clothes.'

Xave say, 'Christmas clothes? I never had that.'

'Your dad didn't buy you Christmas clothes and shoes!?'

She said no.

'Dr. Sebi?'

I come out. 'What happened?'

'You never buy Xave Christmas clothes?'

'Look ma'am, please, just quit.'

"She didn't know. Helen Perkins came. She's a schoolteacher in Boston, a very good teacher for school there. She saw my little girl playing with stuffed animals. So my little girl put the giraffe, the lion, and the rhinoceros over here. Over here she put a hog, a horse, and a cow. So, Helen Perkins asked my daughter,

'Why have you separated the animals when all animals are alike?'

My daughter said no.

Now remember, this lady is teaching the children in school in Boston. My daughter put the stuff back over here.

'Why do you separate them?'

She said, 'Because these animals are unnatural. They need a vet. All unnatural animals need a vet. A dog need a vet. A cat needs a vet. A cow needs a vet. Every animal that is unnatural needs a vet. But these animals,' she said, 'over here, lions need no vet, neither does a gorilla, or rhinoceros, and giraffes. They don't need vets. Why? They are natural.'[5]

"They have been made with all of their immune system intact," Sebi says. "The woman said, 'I never heard of that.' My daughter picked up the animals and went outside and played with the rest of the children and forget about Helen Perkins. Helen Perkins felt insulted. But my little girl didn't have the time to educate a teacher. My little girl was only nine. When Xave got to sixteen, she said,

'Dad, I want to go to school.'

I said, 'Oh God, oh my God.' I was so hurt. Look, I felt like I failed my little girl. Where did I fail, that my little girl wants to go to school? I said,

'Why you want to go to school?'

She said, 'Well, you see, I don't have any friends. I don't have any friends. And I'm going to meet friends in school.'

I said, 'But you're sixteen. I'm not going to take you to school and register you in school. No, I'm not going to do that.' She asked her mother. Her mother said, 'Hell no.'

"You know what Xave did? She took the keys, got the car, because she already had the license at fourteen, passed the test in L.A., went to the school, on Berryman Avenue in L.A., right off of Jefferson. And she registered herself in school. The school teacher said,

'Where's your mother and father?'

'Well, they are not here. They are at work.' Okay, fill this sheet out, the form, the uh, what do you call it now, to enter school?" Sebi asks his audience. They reply application.

"Right. While my little daughter is filling it out the teacher asked her,

'Where is your transcript?'

My daughter said, 'Transcript? What's that?'

Right there, my daughter didn't know anything about transcripts. But some that have been conditioned knows about transcripts. Not my daughter. She told my daughter the transcript is the works of your last school, the papers with your grades and all that stuff.

Xave said, 'Well I never been to school.'

'You never been to school? How did you fill this out?'

She said, 'That's easy.'

The teacher said, 'What you mean easy?'

"The teacher didn't know. The teacher had no idea. She never communicated or he never communicated with a child that's never been to school. So now he's going to be very surprised because he thought that when the school educates you, you're on top of things. You know everything. Oh yeah? You don't know the world. And it went on to a little heavier test. When my child was examined, because she's sixteen, you have to be in grade what, ten? Tenth grade, right? They gave her the exam, and she came out with A plus, plus, plus, plus, plus. So they had to accept her. But now they are puzzled. They are puzzled because how could this child not go to school and she could excel? After being in school for six months, all hell is going to break loose. They gave my little girl a multi—you know those questionnaires where you have multi, multiple-choice exam.

"Protein. Deficit or equity? Xave put deficit. The teacher came back and say,

'Xave you never make mistakes. Why did you make this one?'

My daughter say, 'Which one?'

'You chose, you put deficit for protein.'

Xave say, 'Is that a mistake?'

'Of course,' the teacher say. And remember now, this man is teaching high school in the United States. But then again, the United States is number twelve on the educational standards in the world.[6] So what do you expect? They're not number one, number two, number three, number ten. They're number twelve. But an American too, doesn't know that. And it so happen to be that the number one in the world for academic accomplishment is Barbados. Always number one!" Sebi says emphatically. "Not America, not Germany, not England. Barbados!"[7]

"The teacher said, 'You put deficit.'

Xave said yes.

'But that's wrong.'

'Why is it wrong?' my daughter said. 'Do you agree that the human body is carbon-based?'

He said yes.

'Well, would you agree that the food that's going to feed a carbon-based body has to like-wise be carbon-based?'

He said yes.

'But teacher,' she said, 'carbon-based substances are all electrical.'

He said yes."

Sebi stops telling the story to explain electricity's connection to carbon. "You get electricity from carbon, right? Even those solar panels, it better be carbon in there. You cannot derive electricity unless it has a carbon base. Impossible! You cannot do that. So my daughter said,

'Well if it's carbon-based, it's electrical.'

He said yes.

My daughter asked him how many electrons per atom does protein contain? Holy Christ. I know for a fact that there aren't any professors in the United States that have had that question posed to them by a student. But because I'm her father I would sit with her every day and spend at least four hours with my daughter and her mother, you know, to show her carbon, hydrogen, and oxygen. If you call my daughter right now," he says, referring to Saama, his youngest daughter born in Honduras and also educated by him, "and go to the room and bring her here and ask her, 'Saama, what are the components of life? What is the base, the basic components of life?' She'll tell you carbon, hydrogen, and oxygen."

Sebi concludes the story, telling his guests Xave eventually dropped out of school.

"My daughter now is running my business," he says. "She made all the compounds you all are taking. You all may not know that. My daughter, she's twenty-four years of age. That is us. You could do it. You, you, you and all of us in here. But Xave having parents like us, she was lucky because my wife is antischool. So am I. But if she had a parent that was proschool she would not have ever learned those things, right? Impossible.

"So it is the central nerve system that has been completely destroyed. I mean, we so nervous that we talk out of turn. We anticipate what someone else is going to say and we behave erratic. And I be looking at it. And boy, I realize that, like my mother told me, you are not in a position to criticize anyone. I said, 'Why?' Because you're not. Because you know better. So when you know better, you're like the teacher and the student. The teacher now have to teach the student that doesn't know. So he cannot be angry at the student, right?

"I used to get angry. I used to go on stage in D.C. You don't want to see my lectures in D.C. They were volatile! They were explosive. 'Dr. Sebi! You said we shouldn't drink carrot juice.' I would go off on you. I would go off on you. I would practically insult you. I may cuss you out. Why would I do that? I used to wonder why was I so volatile against the people that's in front of me. Why? Because what one gorilla knows, all gorillas know," Sebi stresses to his audience in Usha's dining room. "So I want to know how come I know this and you don't. I didn't like that. I felt insecure. I felt very insecure. I used to get angry at you when you didn't know. They interpret it like I was angry. No, I was very much disturbed because you didn't know, and you are my sister and my brother. The more of us that knows, the safer it is for all of us.

"I told my momma, 'Look, I'm not going to spend my life educating the world and what they should know. Then what's going to happen to me?' I have to find an environment where I can save myself because I'm happy. What you have to do is to see Sebi in his environment and accept Sebi in his environment and hope that you will develop yours. Because Sebi has to live that. Many people come here, and they will even say, 'I can't see why he's able to cure people. He smokes marijuana. He uses profanity. He just don't give a damn.' Oh, what does that have to do with me knowing something?" He repeats his rhetorical question. "What does that have to do with me knowing something?"

Sebi did give a damn. He was not a fly-by-night angry black man. At first glance, people new to his persona might think so. Yet Sebi was not. He was a self-taught natural healer. He was brilliant, but I'm hesitant to use that word because Sebi didn't embrace labels, other than words like "sick," "healthy," "natural," "hybrid," "resonance." He'd tell you he's not weak or strong. He's not rich or poor. He just lives. Labels were not his thing. A woman Sebi and I know, Pamela Ferrell of Cornrows & Co., calls him "brilliant." Pamela and I discussed titles for this book. One of her suggestions included the word brilliant, referring to Sebi's brilliant work in herbal healing. But since I knew Sebi's feeling about such words, I chose the book's current title, *Dr. Sebi Speaks of Dembali*, and I'm pleased with the choice. However, looking back at those brainstorming meetings with Pamela, I have to concede that Sebi was indeed brilliant. The evidence I give is his love affair and achievements with plants and herbs, an affinity as strong as that of botanist and agriculturist George Washington Carver. Sebi did more than go to an open field, look at plants, grab one or two, and take them back to his kitchen, mix them in a pot with other plants, pour them in jars, and then give the compounds to us. Sebi made sure his products contained top-quality natural plants. Of course, to Sebi, any plant nature makes has a purpose and is top quality—second to none.

He sent his herbs to Lancaster Laboratories (now Eurofins Lancaster Laboratories) in Pennsylvania, a facility that tests the authenticity and efficacy of plants and other items in various industries. Lancaster tested Sebi's products for their alkaline properties. It verified and confirmed that Sebi's herbal compounds were 100 percent natural, alkaline, vegetation cell food.

In the Land of Krishna and Buddha

Further evidence of Sebi's brilliance is his friendship with people like Chakravarti Rajagopalachari, governor-general of India during the country's independence movement. According to *India Today* magazine, he was "one of the most influential leaders of India." He was an editor, statesman, and lawyer. He formed the Tamil Scientific Terms Society, an organization that translated scientific terms of chemistry, physics, mathematics, astronomy, and biology into simple Tamil words. On a humanitarian note, one that shows how men like Sebi and Rajagopalachari could become friends, in 1939, as premier of the Madras Presidency, Rajagopalachari issued the Temple Entry Authorization and Indemnity Act. It allowed Dalits and Shanars (India's untouchables) to enter temples. *India Today* wrote, "This was a major boost to abolish untouchability and caste prejudice" in the eastern Indian state of Tamil Nadu on the Bay of Bengal. Lucky for Rajagopalachari he wasn't a guru, I discover one evening when Sebi and I talk about African resonance and how it compares to other cultures.

"In the world today, especially India," Sebi says as he begins his discussion of the relationship between America and gurus for his audience, "America has been bombarded with Indians, you know. And I remember when there were no Indian gurus in America. Remember, I live in America since 1954. How many years that's been? Fifty what? Fifty-four, right? Older than you guys, some of you," he says to his guests in the dining room. "So I've been looking. I wasn't asleep. I was looking when everybody

USHA VILLAGE 2008—DR. SEBI, HIS GUESTS, AND DEMBALI

was reading. I was looking. America didn't have gurus. America begin to invite gurus to come to America from India. And they came saying, 'Love, love is the ultimate pursuit. It is love that brings compassion. It is love, and it is love.' Tell that to a man that's eating a hog's head. Preach to a man that's eating chitlins and hog maw about love. The very food he's eating is undermining the individual to have the ability to reach this love thing this Indian is talking about. In 1960, I was in India and there was a great big occurrence in '60 that took place between Burma, India, China, and Kathmandu, Nepal. What was that? The Chinese went into Kathmandu, Nepal, and destroyed practically every edifice that Buddha represented. What did the Dalai Lama have to do? He had to leave Kathmandu and run to Burma.

"I was in India. There's a little boy who used to come to my hotel and hear me talk to people. He said,

'You think you smart but you ain't smart. I know a man smarter than you.'

I said, 'Yeah?'

'Well, I'm going to bring him.'

So he brought this Indian named Rajagopalachari. Bad dude. I mean the baddest I ever met. So Rajaji said,

'I came to meet the wise man.'

I said, 'If you are wise as the young man said, and I'm wise, you already know that I don't know anything.'" Sebi chuckles.

Sebi and Rajagopalachari became close friends. They traveled together to Rangoon, Burma, to meet the Dalai Lama. Sebi recounts the story.

"The Dalai Lama had all these people around him. Oh, he was preaching about love. I go in there and they have all these people around this Dalai Lama. But nobody's saying anything. How in the hell they know this boy have something in his skull? I'm gonna find out. So Rajaji doesn't want me to do my mischievousness. But, hold it. Nobody owns me. Nobody owns my thoughts. So I asked, 'My most humble and distinguished sir, I would like to ask where did you go in the universe to retrieve this wisdom that suffice all, when everybody on the planet is like a leaf on a tree—unique, unlike the other? How were you able to find wisdom to suffice all?'

"If the man was an herbalist I could understand. But the man is using words. I said, 'Where do you get this wisdom that suffice all?' He did this. He hanged his head. I let one minute pass. Two minutes passed. And he's gonna seek a refuge. I said, 'Sir I'm leaving, back to Calcutta, India.' Calcutta is not too far from Rangoon. I said, 'I have to go back to Calcutta and I'm leaving. Do I get a response?' Guess what he said? 'I have answered you.' I said, 'With silence.'

"I walked out the pagoda. Behind me is a Frenchman and a German. They were so angry. But if you look carefully in America and in Europe, it's these Europeans who push these gurus, right? And they behind them like they really God. So the Frenchman came and told me,

'He could have answered you. He could have answered you.'

This Frenchman didn't know who he was talking to. This Frenchman thought I was an African out of Cote d'Ivoire. No, uh-un. I'm that black man that was never conditioned. So I looked at him. I said, 'What did you say Pierre?'

'He could have answered you.'

I didn't need his answer. Because when Nature made me, Nature put me in Africa. Nature didn't put me in Africa void of a component that I have to fly all the way across to Kathmandu, Nepal, to find the other part of me. When Nature put me in Africa, Nature endowed me with everything that I needed. That man didn't have any answer for me.

USHA VILLAGE 2008—DR. SEBI, HIS GUESTS, AND DEMBALI

"So now, when we leave here, check yourself. Check yourself. Or else you will never grow. When you come in contact with another individual, just look in his eyes and listen. Just listen. Please, listen. And listen. Because we have been conditioned. We are zombies."

Sebi's guests do listen, fixated on every one of his statements. The camera picks it up when I turn the lens away from Sebi and pan the faces of the eight men and women in the dining room. They listen and stare, barely blinking. Even the Honduran sun that beams through the windows warming shoulders and faces fails to interrupt the stillness. But what's unaffected by the calm are the demonstrative hands Sebi uses to drive his points home, one point in particular is the central nervous system's role in conditioning.

"When I said that what we eat destroys the central nerve system, what do we eat?" he asks the group. "All hybrid food. I don't need to go into that part but the other part I need to go into, when I said that what they make, what they allow us to eat destroys what? The central nerve system. Once they get your central nerve system, they got you for life. Like they got the Pavlovian dog. One day the dog came and there was no milk. He salivated himself to death. How do hybrid plants come into being? Easy. I always use this example because I have to use it in Washington and New York and all over. Men began to take God's product—it started in England with a Jesuit priest named Gregor Mendel.[8] Go to your computer and you're going to see Gregor Mendel. He was a Jesuit priest. He began to experiment with what God made.[9] Like if you take a horse and a jackass and bring them together, you don't make a horse nor a jackass. You make a mule. But you never know what the outcome of these two animals is going to be. That's with the animals."

Origins of Disease

Morning turns to early afternoon at Usha. The temperature rises about five hot degrees. Buttocks shift in seats, but other than that, guests show no sign of disinterest. In the following passage, I remove my narrator's hat. I can only walk a short distance in Sebi's African diaspora-traveled shoes, for his was a life that covered much ground. Sebi is a good storyteller. He sits in the high-back wooden chair in front of his guests. He tells stories of conditioned responses, generational behaviors, and his grandfather's boat better than I ever could. He continues his recollections with an experience in Upstate New York, where he traveled with a group of his clients in the 1980s.

"In New York there's some mountains, the Phoenicia. It's up in the Cascade Mountains. So I took a group of brothers and sisters. The woman who ran the Phoenicia place is a Jewish woman. When we got there that night, around six in the evening, six or seven o'clock, she called me. She said,

'Come. I want to talk to you. I heard about you. You are very particular about things. You are very this and very that. Well, I'm going to give you my menu before the day come, before tomorrow, see if you're satisfied.'

"When I read the woman menu and what she's going to feed the people I took there, it was all in place. Everything was in place. It was good. I said, 'You pass the test or else I'll put them back on the bus and take them back to New York.' Now, the next day I'm supposed to begin to work with these people. I don't have any set ways of delineating something like, 'Well, I'm going to take these people to New York, in the mountains, and my program is going to be that, that, that, that, that.' It never works out. I don't do that. So I go, I took them down in a barn five o'clock next day to show them the breathing exercise that we need to learn to revitalize ourselves. After they did that, everybody was like, 'Wow Dr. Sebi! I got so much energy all of a sudden.' So they all sit down in front of me. I stood up and I looked at them and took a while. And now they are so nervous that a brother asked, 'What are you looking for?' I say, 'Why do you ask what are you looking for?' Why would he even ask that question?

"You know something, brothers and sisters, I didn't know what I was looking for. I was just looking at them. Finally, in a second it came. I said, 'You all know what I'm looking for? I'm looking for the ugliest person in the audience.' Look, everybody slumped. I said, 'The ugliest person better stand up, and come up here with me.' Nobody stood up. I don't know why they didn't stand up. I said, 'You, young lady.' I could have chosen anyone, because that's how we all feel. So she came up here and she stood by me. I left her standing right there, and went and sat where she did. I said, 'Now, young lady I want you to tell us what part of you and what area of you you dislike. And she start crying. She cried and she cried and she cried. And when she got out of crying she said,

'When I was a little girl my mother told me this, and my daddy said this to me, and the neighbors said this. And I believed it, and I grew up that way. Now I'm twenty-seven and I still feel that.'

"That's how cruel we are. But the rest of the folks that were there ran up and rescued her in her crying. Her boyfriend asked me,

'How did you know that my girlfriend needed that kind of therapy?'

I said, 'Because you need it too. Everybody there needed it. I only selected her. I watched every one of you here right now. And I could tell each and every one of you who is the most nervous. I could see. You see, I didn't read books to relate to you. I use my eyes to relate to you, my senses, my brain. Books cannot prepare you to do that kind of therapy I just performed with those people. That doesn't come out of a book. The healing I bring to you, brothers and sisters doesn't come out of a book either, because if it was in a book why are you here? All you have to do is go buy the book, right? And you wouldn't need to come to see Sebi. But it is not in a book. It isn't a book. And Junior Lion sings. He doesn't sing like Marley. He doesn't sing like Peter Tosh. But he sings like Junior Lion, independent to Tosh and everybody else and Marley. Why? Because he comes with a different resonance and a different message. You understand? And that is something that we have not learned to respect yet. No, we haven't. We have not learned to respect that area of the individual. And when you begin to learn to respect that, you begin to show prudence. Prudence.

"My grandfather, lucky for me, because I didn't go to school, my grandfather was a man that did things in Roatán they still talk about now. First of all, he made his coffin fifteen years before he died. He made his own coffin, and sometimes he would sleep in it. He would talk to it. 'Hey boy, I'm not ready yet, okay?' He made his coffin and put it in the ceiling where he can look at it. Grandfather did something, though. He made a boat, named the *Suzy S*, and everybody came and said,

'Uncle Wally, the timber is too thin. You should make it thicker.'

'The timbers are too small. You should make them larger.'

'The mast is too short. Make it taller.'

My grandmother Sarah, the day that they are going to christen the boat, she came with the bottle of alcohol, and she gonna slap the boat, and they gonna release the boat in the water. The boat went straight to the bottom. Everybody said,

'Oh, Uncle Wally boat sunk. Uncle Wally boat sunk.'

My grandfather said, 'What did you say? That *my* boat sunk!? No. My boat didn't sink, because you haven't seen my boat yet. This boat that sunk is the people's boat!'

"Everybody came and gave my grandfather advice, like Beverly did, telling me I should paint the fence brown or green. That is not what I want to do. But Beverly didn't know that. I mean, I was watching her day before yesterday telling me what color to paint, and I remember my grandfather. My grandfather said,

'I'm going to make a boat now.' And when he started the other boat, he didn't raise the boat out of the water. He left it right there. As he start the second boat, there was someone that came, and my grandfather said, 'Wait! The boat that everybody had shares in is under the water. This is going to be Wallace Bowman boat.'

"That's the way I live. That glass house over there, they never seen a glass house like that in their life in Honduras. I don't think anywhere else in the world."

Sebi started building his new residence at Usha, a circular two-story glass structure, in 2008, and as of the publishing of this book, that phenomenal, genius of an architectural design still stands.

"But I made a mistake," he continues. "I made a mistake. I goes in town and I tell my friend I'm gonna build a glass house. 'Who? You gonna do what!?' Matun nudged me. She said, 'You're stupid. You acting stupid, boy. Come on. Let's go back to the village. Don't tell nobody anything else because it's going to happen like your grandfather, and you're going to get angry at them. Build the house without the recommendation of anyone.' And now when they see the house, they go, 'Wow, what a pretty house.' But the house is already built, right? That's the way we have to conduct ourselves—respecting the views of another. The respect of the opinion of others or the right of others is peace. The respect of the rights of others is what?" The audience responds 'peace.'

"You know who built this village? I did. You know who designed those huts? I did. I like to say I did. Why not? But in America they call that selfishness." He enunciates every syllable of the word, drawing it out.

"Oh yeah? But who lives in here with me? Tell me. Who lives inside of Sebi? Who lives inside of Sebi, with Sebi? Nobody, right? So, as I see and I talk, it's not selfishness. It's unique to me. It's all selfishness. You are too. You are and all of us here. But we don't respect those boundaries. This is why my office saw me going through frustration in the last, in the last couple of—let me say the last twelve years. They saw me going up and down with emotion. And they said, 'Sebi, you live unlike anybody we know. So, what we're going to do to avoid you from going up these upheavals, up and down, we're going to separate you from the world, that you can live in your world quietly. The only thing that you're going to do is give lectures. You're not going to see any more sick people. Never again.' I said, 'But who is going to handle the business?' 'We're going to do it.' And guess what? They're doing a better job than me. They're doing a much better job than me.

"My mother told me, 'You have to write the book.' I said, 'No, Momma. I'm not going to write any book.' She said, 'Why?' I said, 'Because the black man of America have a million books in front of his face. Why does he need another one?' 'Ah, it's not your book that you're going to write. You're going to write what nature is showing us that we don't know. And we need to know. It's not your book.'

"That's why I was encouraged to ask Beverly to come and write the first book. That's the only reason why. So please, remember your nerves. Your nerve is what causes you to see things differently. When I saw Sanjee, Sanjee was shaking like a leaf the night when he came. I couldn't understand why. But I know his nerve was shattered."

Sebi points to Sanjee's partner. "Now, she said to me yesterday, 'Wow, Sanjee went in the bath and he's calm.' She told me he was the last one left last night, right?" He chuckles and recalls the gathering in his cabin the night before his lecture. "You see. I was asleep. Tell me, what have you learned since you've been here? What do you see? What manifested?"

Someone from the audience responds off mic. "You seldom see smiling faces."

"You mean among us? Oh wow. You see that?" Sebi says, wrapping up his talk. It's the first time I've seen him ask an audience for feedback right on the spot. There are usually questions and answers from the audience, rarely an evaluation. Dembali, did they get it?

"What about you my brother?" he asks a young man from Jamaica. "Since you've been here, what is it that you see overall? Extrapolate something that was out of the ordinary that you saw here, that you feel here."

"Peace of mind," he answers.

"Unconditional love," a young lady adds.

"Oh, that is beautiful," Sebi says. "That makes me feel good. What about you young lady?"

A woman from England replies, "I'm seeing the surroundings. For me, it's something that I have never seen before. But I've been to Antigua and the environment is like this, but the surroundings here, for me, that in itself is like a therapy. It's tranquil and peaceful."

"Well, I don't think that I could ask Sanjee. He just got here. But he got a smile on his face, which I like. And I know that

Sanjee has received already at least a degree of something good. Right? Now, do you know that each of you gave a response that shows something very nice?" Sebi asks.

Back to Ease

Sebi's last demonstration of a transition from dis-ease to ease is the story of four men, including himself, and how each man pursues peace, dignity, health, and community activism.

"A Mexican came here one day. The Mexican came and I got my pants rolled up, and I'm sittin' under the mango tree, bare feet under the mango tree over there. The Mexican came and looked at the place. He said, talking to me, didn't know who I am or was. He said,

'The man that built this place must be a peaceful individual.'

I said, 'I hope he is sir.' Because I let him think that I was not the owner or anything. He said,

'The man that made this place must be peaceful.'

I said, 'I hope that he is.'

He said, 'I'm going to come here one day. I just came. I heard about this place, and they said that Dr. Sebi is the doctor that tend to people.'

I said, 'Yes, he's the man that tend to people.'

He said, 'The man must be peaceful. This place is nice.'

"And he left. But listen to this. Soon thereafter, a Japanese came with an entourage. And then he had these black cars come in the gate. I'm sitting under the mango tree. So they walked over there. He saw me with my pants rolled up, because I like to roll my pants up. I don't know, think I got that from my uncle. Winston was a man that never wore shoes in his life. He died at eighty-two, never wore shoes in his life. I don't know how women liked him, because he never wore shoes." Sebi laughs.

USHA VILLAGE 2008—DR. SEBI, HIS GUESTS, AND DEMBALI

"My uncle didn't care about shoes, my grandfather either. So they're sitting underneath the mango tree with me. These are Japanese. He said, without even thinking, because nobody in the world live a nervous life like a Japanese. Japanese students blow their brains out by the thousands a month. That's why the Viento is going to sell in Japan big time, because a Japanese man took it to Japan, and what he saw he couldn't believe. Japanese students blow their brains out because they are forced to excel.[10] But as you take a look at the Japanese food you could see why they're nervous, right? Look at what they eat. Rice. Rice. And more rice. It's such a detrimental thing that Dr. Ohsawa, do you all know who Dr. Ohsawa is? (George Ohsawa) Dr. Ohsawa is a Japanese that came out with a diet that you guys know of, the macrobiotic diet.[11] What is at the base of the macrobiotic diet? Rice. Rice. And more rice.[12]

"The Japanese goes and he tells me, 'Go tell the boss that I want to talk to him.'

So I had a little child's bicycle, a child that used to visit me from across the street. I jumped on the little bicycle, you know, and I rode and I came back.

I said, 'Sir, the boss wants to know what do you want with him?'"

Sebi's guests laugh. "I had to do that because I could see the man was nervous, so I have to play, do something to treat this man because this man is nervous. This man didn't ask me or introduce himself—'Hi, my name is so and so and so. Well, my name is so and so. I heard about this place and it's very nice, and do you work here? Who are you?' No! He automatically assumed that I was the yard boy. I jumped on the bicycle and I rode around. I'm gonna fix him, right? So I came back. I said, 'The boss says what do you want with him?'

'I want to tell the boss that I want to buy this place.'

I go and come back. 'The boss says he don't think he want to sell it.'

He said, 'Well, I want to see the boss.'

I said, 'You're looking at him.' He didn't know what to say. He didn't know what to say because he compromised his own self. But we're so accustomed in opening our mouth, we talk out of turn. We just believe, we make emphasis, we assume, we philosophize, and we rationalize everything, even though it's wrong. That's us. That's what they did to us—destroy our central nerve system, so much so that my wife sister told her, 'Your daughter is going to amount to nothing because she's not going to school.' My wife mother told her, 'You are raising a dunce because she's not going to school.' Look at Xave. Xave curing AIDS. Xave cured a blind woman in New York. Tell that to a medical science student.

"This is why sisters, Dr. Sebi is putting together a cadre, a cadre of sisters, no brothers. No. You are not going to participate in the healing. Where we will participate is in the hard construction." Sebi looks at Junior Lion, the reggae artist. "You the farmer. You bad, they tell me. I like that. I have a brother in St. Croix named Lumumba, also Rasta man. Bad dude. He knows how to farm. I don't know how to farm. You know. So all of us males are going to do the work that would enhance the sisters' healing."

The healing project Sebi speaks of targets black communities in the United States initially, then branches out to international communities. Sebi designed it to help black people return to their original self-sufficient selves in farming, clothes-making, and natural health. He shared the proposal for the $300-million project with some of the guests in his cabin the previous night. He continues the conversation with the rest of us in the dining room, telling us the project's initial investment would be $92 million.

"When you talk like this, to the general public, in Atlanta, hey, you try it when you get back to Atlanta—if you could get across town, because you have lines now to buy gasoline. When you go across town, tell your friends, 'You know, I am a part of a $300-million project.' They'll say, 'Oh girl, shut up.' What are they going to do? You're putting a wrench in it now. It's impossible, right? And all it costs is $300 per person. Once in your life. There would be $300 million. There's two ships cost $10 million. There's the agricultural land, which is a thousand acres, $2 million. There's five buildings in New York, Chicago, Atlanta, Los Angeles, and San Francisco. Five buildings, $25 million. Five farms because there are brothers in America that know how to farm. The brothers in the United States around Bakersfield, South Carolina, also around Illinois. I met them myself because I did my research to see if this was possible. These brothers know how to grow stuff. They say, 'Sebi we would grow what you want organically.' And we would have these buildings in which these things would be sold out of, right? So we're going to give each brother, how much we said? There's five farmers, and there's $10 million—$2 million dollars per brother. That's right. How do you think that brother is going to feel when we put $2 million in his hand to refurbish his farm and grow the organic food to supply our centers? Isn't that love? Isn't that beauty? Of course it is.

"So, as we stop and we look at this dembali project, this $300-million project, included is this [Usha Village]. This is part of it. This project would own this. Sebi would not own this village. Sebi have no right to own this village. That's not even right. Brother Sebi own healing? No. Dr. Sebi own the village of Usha? Why not say *we* own it? We own Usha. I want you all to show me something now, if I'm so wrong. Where in the world do we go in America, Africa, or the Caribbean, and here in Central America where I'm from, where do we go and find a meaningful project that was developed by us? And those of us that do to some degree, a little degree of something physical, he knows the man. I know him well. The Nuwaubians. Malachi York.[13] I knew Malachi. Me and Malachi were in Islam. I got a picture where Malachi was standing there with me and Malcolm [Malcolm X] and him. But Malachi didn't have my brain. My brain is never to offend you. Malachi York put an organization together on a piece of land that wasn't even clear. Me? I bought this. We could buy our land. He didn't. He wanted the land to be given to him by such and such a state. You know, 'We have to go to the state, you know, ask the state for help.' You done compromise yourself. How come I didn't ask the state for help here? And if I and these two women, Maa and Matun, made this, imagine—Sebi counts people in the dining room—one, two, three, four, five, six, seven, eight, nine, ten. If three people did this, imagine what ten could do.

"Could you give us $300 to bring this about, into reality, where we are going to feed ourselves and house our own folks, our elderly, our elderly that need help? Once we get this money, we could amplify this all the way to the mountain. And you know that in every community in the United States, there are people, elderly, and in England too, that doesn't have any money because the welfare that the state gives our parents and the elderly can't even pay their medicine. Can't even buy adequate food. Can't even live in a place that is decent. How I know that? Well, I'm going to lay it down now. And this the last part.

"I'm in New York, a Monday. My place never open on Monday, whether in L.A. or anywhere in the world. The phone rings on a Monday. I say, 'I'm not going to answer this stupid phone.' The phone ringing. It stopped ringing and ring again. I said, 'Oh God, this must be some emergency.' I pick up the phone.

'Dr. Sebi?'

'Yes.'

'Dr. Sebi, oh, I'm glad you're speaking to me. I'm very sick, Dr. Sebi. I'm very sick. I want you to come and see me.'

I said, 'Okay ma'am. Where you live?'

'I live at 143rd Street and Lenox.'

"And I went. Miss McCadden. When I went to see the lady, she's in bed. I walked up these steps. I walked up this other step and then I go in there. This lady is in her eighties. She laying in bed. The sheet that is supposed to be white is this color." He indicates the light brown on a chair.

"I went with Annette, who was my wife then. There are two people by her bed, one on each side looking at me. And I'm asking her questions. She had rheumatoid arthritis. She was in a very bad way, and she's laying on this bed, and she got a big belly on her, and she's laying on this bed that needs cleaning. So I said, 'Excuse me for a minute. Annette, come here.' I took her outside. I said, 'Annette,'—you know I always have a thousand dollars or more in my pocket all the time—I said, 'I want you to go to the store and buy me two sets of sheets, two sets of pillowcases, two sets of everything you think she needs, even the spread. And I want you to buy some incense and some oils.' And I gave her the money. I gave her $500. I know she came back with some change. So when Annette left, I said 'Please, take her to the bath or bathe her.' And they wiped her down, washed her down in her bed. And then I took the salve, and I rubbed her feet. I massaged her feet with the salve. Guess what Miss McCadden said? 'Wow, I could feel the blood circulating in my feet. Oh, your salve is so good Dr. Sebi. Your salve is so good.' She's feeling better from her legs. Annette came back. They changed the bed. We put the oils on it. And guess what she said when I'm leaving?

'How much I owe you?'

'You owe me $750.'

She took out her coin purse. She said, 'I can give you five dollars down on it.'

I say, 'Miss McCadden, if my momma was standing here and I take your five dollars I think my momma would slap me down and hope that I die. That's okay ma'am. You keep the five dollars, and you use that to buy something else, and please, I may not be here because I'm running up and down the place, Annette will take your name, and Annette will bring you the follow-up.'

"Now, you know how I felt when I went home? And remember, I don't see people on Mondays, right? Because I don't do that. I didn't do that. But when I went home that Monday afternoon, I remember I stopped in Harlem, and I bought some bracelets and I did some things and I went to my room and I lit my joint, smoking my spliff, and thinking about Miss McCadden. I said, 'Look at that. That was so sweet. If I had not gone there, that lady wouldn't be feeling good today.' Out of this project, the many Miss McCaddens that exist in Compton and in Watts and in Harlem, they don't need to be waiting for it. We will send scouts out every month to scout the community to see which and how many Miss McCaddens exist, that we could help. And how much is it going to cost us? Nothing. We have everything here to start an empire, and all it costs is $92 million. But how much is it? Three hundred million dollars. All we spend here is $92 million. So as we leave from here, love doesn't come because you said it, love me or I love you. No, you have to be in a physical state to afford that love to me because when you are in a very helpless state, you cannot even help yourself or give love to yourself. How are you going to give it to me? The Mexican woman showed me that. When she came in the house she was doing this,

'My son brought me here to this barefoot man house and I can't see why he brought me here. This man is dumb. He's bare feet. How is he going to cure me?'

And the son is watching his momma and hearing his momma say that about me. He said, 'I should mention she crazy for eleven years, insane.'

But when she got out of that insane state, when she came back, guess what she had to say? She said,

'I remember you.'

I said yes.

'I cursed you out, right?'

I said yes you did.

She said, 'You know why I cursed you out? You were bare feet. You didn't look like someone who cure people.'

"That brought light on another subject, mind over matter. Caucasians have books that says mind over matter. Am I wrong? Mind over matter. Well, if that is true, where was the lady's mind when she came to see me? What do we say when someone is crazy? 'She lost her mind.' Where was it? She never had it. She never had a mind. You don't have one now. Nobody has a mind. Because if mind was over matter, I don't know what a mind is. You need to go see a doctor that knows about mind, and she did. I went where? To her stomach. And the woman is no longer crazy. So, it's mind over matter? Or matter over mind?"

Epilogue

Occasionally, when Sebi was alive, well, and retired in Honduras, rumors about his death would spread like California wildfires among his supporters. I felt the heat from some of the embers one morning in 2015, when I received a call from Sebi's former assistant, Annette Thomas. I assured her everything was fine—I suppressed all other thoughts—and to prove it, I volunteered to drive to his office on La Cienega Avenue in Los Angeles, to get confirmation from his staff. About five minutes into the trip, Annette called me back to say a friend had heard from Sebi. Another rumor quashed. And just as I dismissed news of his death then, I did it again on August 6, 2016, when friends and relatives offered me condolences in text messages for the passing of my friend Dr. Sebi.

"This is nothing new. It's not true," I replied. But this time, I was wrong. Look on Instagram, they said. Sebi's twenty-one-year-old daughter, Saama, had announced his death there. She was posting from Honduras, where Sebi died.

A few days after the devastation hit me, I drove to Sebi's office, placed my flowers among others under his portrait, and sat for a while. I watched what I presumed were customers and mourners flow in and out of the building, the same building I entered for the first time in 2005.

What I gleaned from my relationship with Dr. Sebi is his courageous support for and homage to African resonance: his muse, his guide, his blueprint for existence, his culling from the past to drive his healing journey. And it seems that on the path, dembali is the lens through which he viewed the human experience. He coined the term to help fill a void not only in black communities—his message speaks volumes for all—but for communities where races and cultures intersect, commingle, and interrelate in matters of health, race, family, and culture. Yet he felt dembali helps black folks most, keeping us grounded, balanced, healthy, and true to Self in the intersection and in our relationship with others. Dembali reminds us to draw from ancestral examples of resiliency and appeals to the cosmos for direction in crossing over back to a state of ease. More often than not, Dr. Sebi said with a roar, "What one gorilla knows, all gorillas know." And when he roared that message, I'm sure Earth nodded, smiled, and rumbled right along with him.

Notes

Chapter One: From the Rainforest to the USA

1. "Health Topics/Female Genital Mutilation," World Health Organization, accessed April 10, 2020, https://who.int.

2. Cynthia Graber, "Snake Oil Salesmen Were on to Something," *Scientific American*, November 1, 2007; Lakshmi Gandhi, "A History of Snake Oil Salesmen," Code Switch: NPR, August 26, 2013.

3. "Iron-Deficiency Anemia," American Society of Hematology, accessed April 17, 2020, http://hematology.org. According to the American Society of Hematology, "Iron is very important in maintaining many body functions, including the production of hemoglobin, the molecule in your blood that carries oxygen...Iron-deficiency anemia is diagnosed by blood tests that should include a complete blood count (CBC). In an individual who is anemic from iron deficiency, these tests usually show the following results: low hemoglobin, low mean cellular volume, low ferritin, low serum iron, high transferrin or total iron-binding capacity, and low iron saturation...Iron deficiency is common in menstruating and pregnant women and others with a diet history of excessive cow's milk (cow's milk not only contains little iron, but it can also decrease absorption of iron and irritate the intestinal lining, causing chronic blood loss) and low iron-containing foods. Symptoms of iron-deficiency anemia are related to decreased oxygen delivery to the entire system."

4. Paavo Airola, *How to Get Well: Dr. Airola's Handbook of Natural Healing* (Phoenix: Health Plus Publishers, 1980), 189.

Chapter Two: On Matters of Race

1. Vasant Joshi, *OSHO: The Luminous Rebel: Story of a Maverick Mystic* (New Delhi: Wisdom Tree Publishers, 2015), Scribd 204, 207.

2. "Bhagwan Shree Rajneesh," The Oregon History Project: A Project of the Oregon Historical Society, accessed April 18, 2020, https://oregonhistoryproject.org/articles/biographies/bhagwan-shree-rajneesh-biography/.

3. Louis Pauwels and Jacques Bergier, *The Morning of the Magicians* (New York: Stein and Day, 1964), 169, 174.

4. Adrian Gilbert and Maurice Cotterell, *The Mayan Prophecies: Unlocking the Secrets of a Lost Civilization* (Boston: Element Books, Inc., 1995), 145, 154.

Chapter Three: On Matters of Culture

1. Jim Thornton, "Is This the Most Dangerous Food for Men?" *Men's Health*, May 19, 2009.

2. K. Shaeer, D.N. Osegbe, S. Siddiqui et al. "Prevalence of erectile dysfunction and its correlates among men attending primary care clinics in three countries: Pakistan, Egypt, and Nigeria," *International Journal of Impotence Research*, 15:S8-S14.

3. Maud Kamatenesi-Mugisha and Hannington Oryem-Origa, "Traditional herbal remedies used in the management of sexual impotence and erectile dysfunction in western Uganda," *African Health Sciences* (2005): 5(1):40-49.

4. Jonathan Hicks, "Reginald F. Lewis, 50, Is Dead; Financier Led Beatrice Takeover," *The New York Times*, January 20, 1993.

Chapter Four: On Matters of Identity

1. George Leone, *Kierkegaard's Existentialism: The Theological Self and the Existential Self* (Indiana: iUniverse, 2014), 10.

NOTES

2. Susan Woolever, "The Process of Self-Becoming in the Thought of Søren Kierkegaard and Carl Rogers," MA (Master of Arts) thesis, University of Iowa, 2013; Søren Kierkegaard, *The Sickness Unto Death* (Macon: Mercer University Press, 1987, originally published 1849), 146, 169-170.

Chapter Five: On Matters of Food and Health

1. Dian Fossey, *Gorillas in the Mist* (Boston: Houghton Mifflin Company, 1983), 49-51.

2. Pamela S. Turner, *Gorilla Doctors: Saving Endangered Great Apes* (New York: Houghton Mifflin Harcourt, 2005), Scribd 27, 40.

3. Board of Science and Technology for International Development, "Lost Crops of Africa; Volume I, Grains" (Washington, DC: National Academy of Sciences, 1996), 1-15.

4. Kathryn Harkup, "Cassava crisis: the deadly food that doubles as a vital Venezuelan crop," *The Guardian*, June 22, 2017.

5. Tim Hartford, "How do people learn to cook a poisonous plant safely?" *BBC News*, September 4, 2019, accessed April 24, 2020, https://bbc.co.uk.

6. Phoebe H. Alitubeera, Patricia Eyu, Benon Kwesiga, Alex R. Ario, Bao-Ping Zhu, "Outbreak of Cyanide Poisoning Caused by Consumption of Cassava Flour—Kasese District, Uganda, September 2017," *Morbidity and Mortality Weekly Report*, Centers for Disease Control and Intervention, April 5, 2019.

7. John Worobey, Beverly J. Tepper, and Robin Kanarek, *Nutrition and Behavior: A Multidisciplinary Approach* (Cambridge: CABI Publishing, 2006), 25, 51, 81.

Chapter Six: Cosmic Arrangement of Life

1. Tim Jones, "Winfrey Distances, and Defends, Herself," *Chicago Tribune*, February 4, 1998.

2. Mark Babineck, "Former USDA Official Slams Oprah," *Associated Press*, January 27, 1988.

3. *Health Culture and Traditional Honduran Indians and Afro-Hondurans* (blog); "Garifuna Medicine—Modern and Traditional, Healers, Doctors, and Medicinal Plants," March 30, 2017.

4. Jules Howard, "Are pets really good for us – or just hairy health hazards?" *The Guardian*, October 13, 2019.

5. Erika Engelhaupt, "How Dog and Cat 'Kisses' Can Turn Deadly," *National Geographic*, October 24, 2017.

Chapter Seven: Usha Village 2008— Dr. Sebi, His Guests, and Dembali

1. Tim Merrill, *Honduras: A Country Study* (Washington, DC: U.S. Library of Congress, 1995), 90.

2. Ian Sample, "Elephant on acid, dog head grafts, and a seesaw to revive the dead," *The Guardian*, November 1, 2007.

3. Daniel Todes, *Ivan Pavlov: Exploring the Animal Machine* (New York: Oxford University Press, 2000), 65, 70-75.

4. Jim Conrad, "Icaco," *Naturalist Newsletter*, May 1, 2011, accessed April 24, 2020, https://www.backyardnature.net/yucatan/icaco.htm.

5. Krista Langlois, "Something Mysterious Is Killing Captive Gorillas," *The Atlantic*, March 5, 2018.

6. Oscar Williams-Grut, "The 11 Best School Systems in the World," *Business Insider*, November 17, 2016.

7. Council on Hemispheric Affairs, "Barbados Ahead of the Pack As the Most Competitive Country in the Caribbean," November 15, 2011.

8. He actually joined the Augustinian friars in Germany, where he trained to be a priest, and while other plant hybridizers existed before him, Mendel became, posthumously, the most renowned. Edward Edelson, *Gregor Mendel and the Roots of Genetics* (UK: Oxford University Press, 1999), 9.

NOTES

9. R.C. Punnett, *Mendelism* (London: MacMillan and Co., Limited, 1911), 7, 15.

10. Stephanie Lu, "Why Do So Many Japanese Schoolchildren Kill Themselves?" *Newsweek*, November 8, 2015; "School issues are No. 1 reason behind youth suicides in 2018, Japanese government white paper finds," *The Japan Times*, July 16, 2019.

11. Menaka Wilhelm, "The Far Out History of How Hippie Food Spread Across America," NPR, January 23, 2018.

12. Lindsay Tucker, "Dial in Your Diet," *Yoga Journal*, July 9, 2018.

13. David S. Menjor, "Who Is Dr. Malachi York?" *Daily Observer*, May 16, 2018.

Bibliography

Aniys, Aqiyl. *Alkaline Herbal Medicine: Reverse Disease and Heal the Electric Body*. North Charleston: Natural Life Energy, LLC, 2016.

Dubois, W. E. Burghardt. *The World and Africa: An Inquiry Into the Part Which Africa Has Played in World History*. New York: International Publishers, 1965.

Locke, Alain. *Negro Art: Past and Present*. Washington, DC: Associates in Negro Folk Education, 1936.

Marino, Gordon, ed. *The Quotable Kierkegaard*. Princeton: Princeton University Press, 2014.

Merrill, Tim. *Honduras: A Country Study*. Washington, DC: U.S. Library of Congress, 1995.

Oliver, Beverly. *Seven Days in Usha Village: A Conversation with Dr. Sebi*. Los Angeles: Dr. Sebi's Office, LLC, 2007.

———. *Sojourn to Honduras Sojourn to Healing: Why An Herbalist's View Matters More Today Than Ever Before*. Los Angeles: JBDavid Communications, 2010.

Pauwels, Louis, and Jacques Bergier. *The Morning of the Magicians*. New York: Stein and Day, 1964.

Rinpoche, Sogyal. *The Tibetan Book of Living and Dying*. New York: HarperCollins Publishers, 1992.

Soyinka, Wole. *Of Africa*. New Haven: Yale University Press, 2012.

Williams, Chancellor. *The Destruction of Black Civilization: Great Issues of a Race from 4500 B.C. to 2000 A.D.* Chicago: Third World Press, 1974.

www.ingramcontent.com/pod-product-compliance
Lightning Source LLC
Chambersburg PA
CBHW021405290426
44108CB00010B/393